It's so easy being green. Your friends will just croak when they see your latest bead creation.

Materials:
Toho 11/0 seed beads (Clear #1, Green #108, Orange #42)
Black plastic beads
7mm White acrylic bead with large hole
10mm White acrylic bead with large hole
Split ring • Head pin • Wire • Key chain • Nylon thread

1. **Frog's head**: Tape 70cm (28") of nylon thread down to work surface 8cm (3") away from the end. Pass thread through 10mm acrylic bead.

2. With taped end at the bottom, string beads on thread, wrapping them around the 10mm bead.

3. Continue stringing beads as in Step 2, paying careful attention to number and color. String beads in direction indicated by arrow. For Rows 4 and 12, see Step 4 Making the ears.
If a large area of the 10mm bead shows through after you've strung the beads for Row 15, add more rows until the bead is covered.

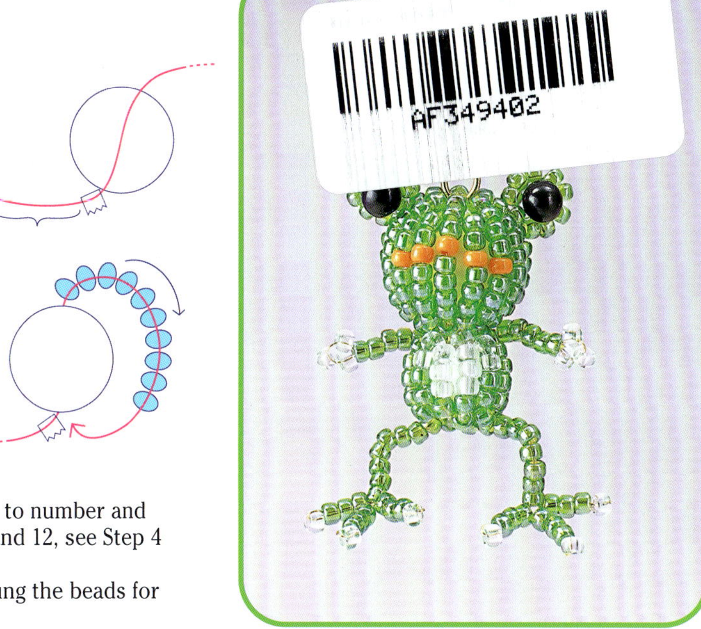

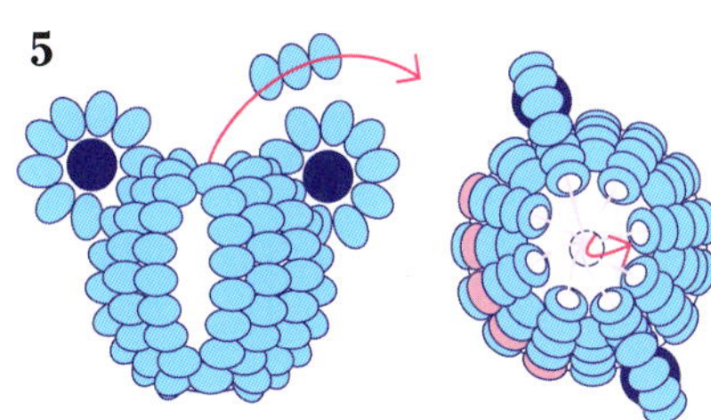

4. **Making the ears:** Add beads. Run thread through bead again. Add beads. Run thread through bead (see diagram). Add beads. Pass thread through acrylic bead. If a large area of the 10mm bead shows through after you've strung the beads for Row 15, add more rows until the bead is covered.

5. After you've strung the beads for the last row, run thread through beads in Row 1. Tie thread to end left at starting point 2-3 times.

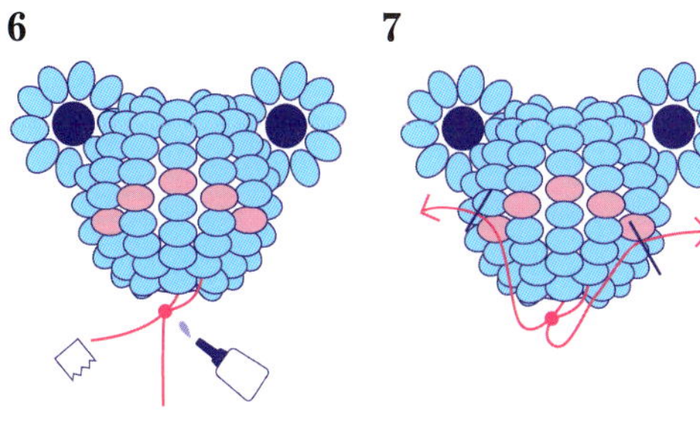

6. Remove tape; apply glue sparingly to knot.

7. Run thread through 2-3 beads; cut excess.

8. **Frog's body:** Use the 7mm acrylic bead and 50cm (20") nylon thread. The body is made in the same way as the head. Legs will be attached in Step 9 (see diagram). After stringing beads for Row 11, finish in same way as Step 5.

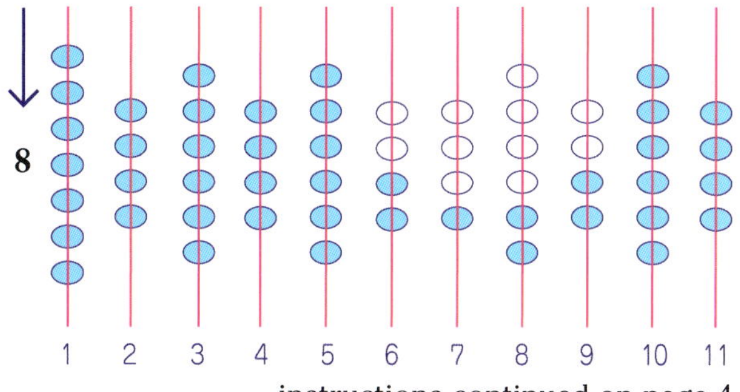

Features of 'Toho' Beads

Large Holes - The size of the holes in Toho beads allows for threading multiple strands of thread or thicker thread, increasing the variety of beadwork you can achieve.

Light Weight - The larger hole means less weight so you get more beads when you buy by weight. There are approximately 111,800 size 11/0 Toho beads per kilogram (2.2 lbs).

Small & Large Round

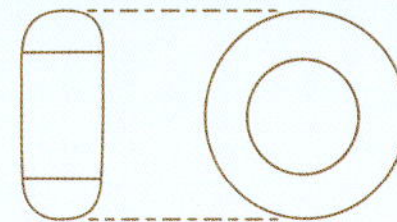

instructions continued on page 4

instructions continued from page 3

9. **Make legs** and attach to body: Fold wire in half and string beads to make hind leg.

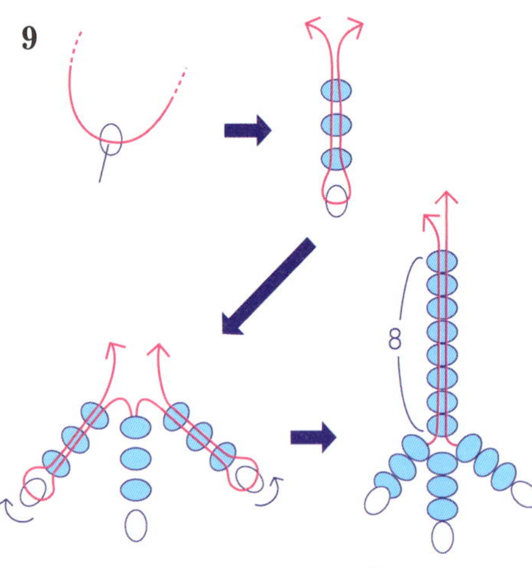

10. Pass one length of wire through Row 4 of beads on body made in Step 8. Pass other length through acrylic bead.

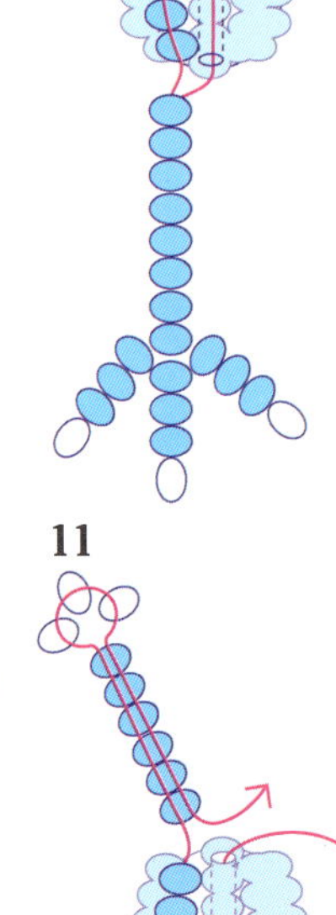

11. String beads on wire extending from Row 4 to make front leg. Set other end of wire aside.

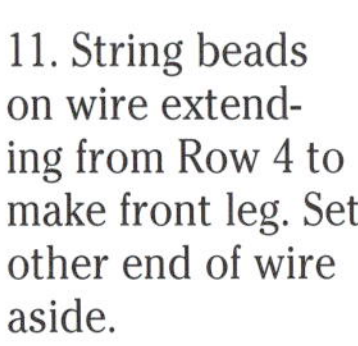

12. Twist the two lengths of wire together. Cut excess wire. After twisting the wire, fold ends under to prevent injury.

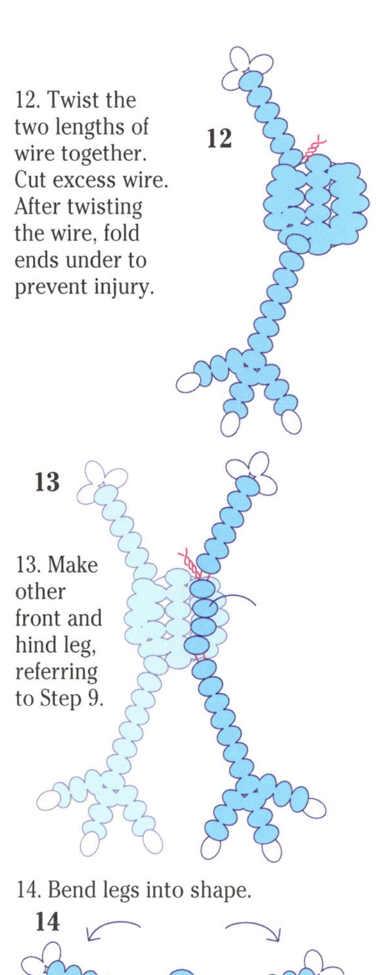

13. Make other front and hind leg, referring to Step 9.

14. Bend legs into shape.

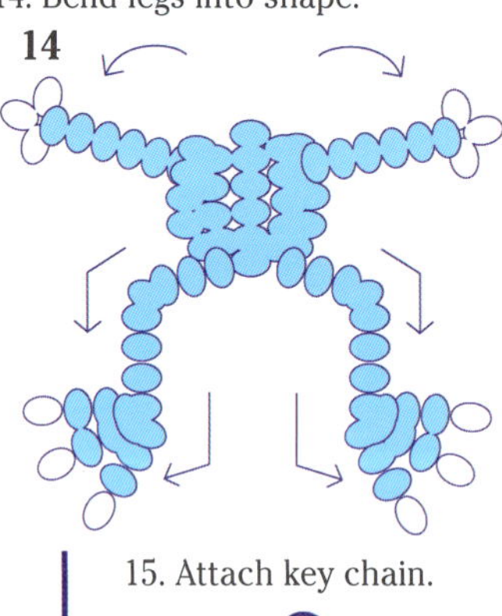

15. Attach key chain.

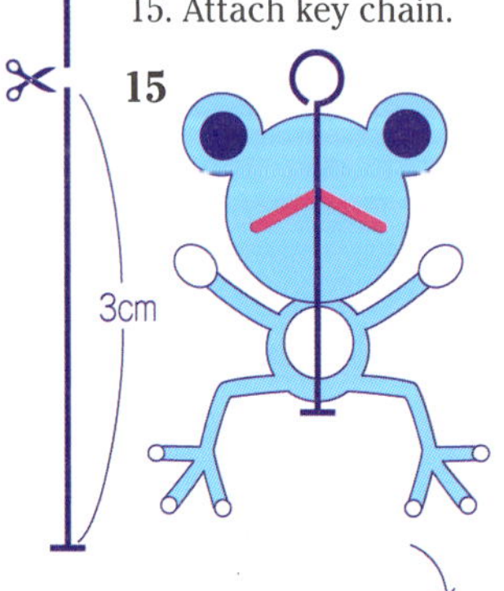

16. See page 2 instructions Using Head Pins and Adding a Split Ring.

Fresh from the forest, this curious raccoon is just looking for a purse or back pack to get into.

Materials:
Toho 11/0 seed beads (Orange #957, White #41, Brown #46)
Toho Black #M49 magatama bead
Toho 3mm Black #PB-313 pop beads 32 Gauge gold wire • Split Ring • Key chain

1. **Raccoon's face**: Cut two 60cm (24") lengths of wire. String beads on one of them, referring to diagrams.

1

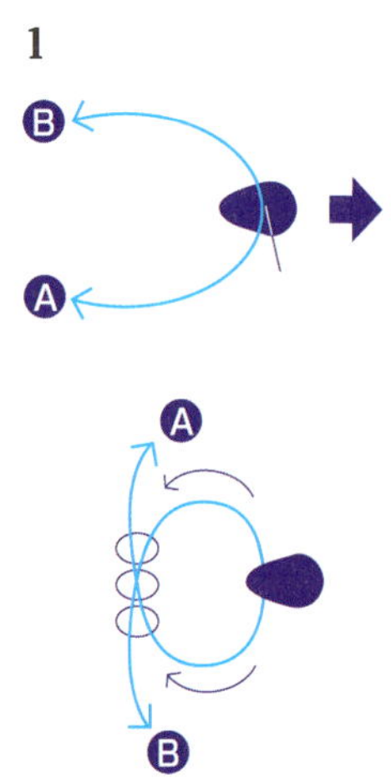

2. String beads on other length wire, referring to diagrams.

2

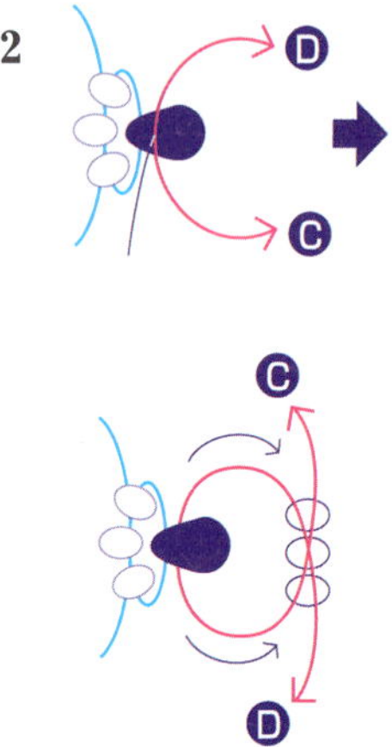

3. Add beads, forming inter-sections as you go.

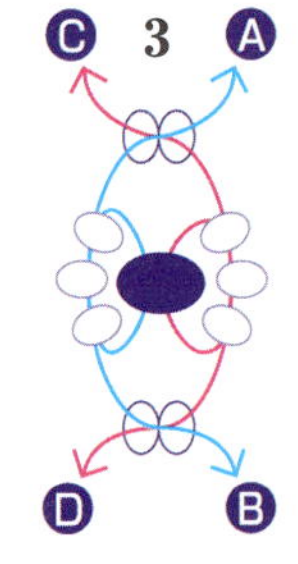

4. Add more beads, forming intersections as you work, to make face. Pull wire so that first bead strung (magatama bead) rises above the plane of the other beads.

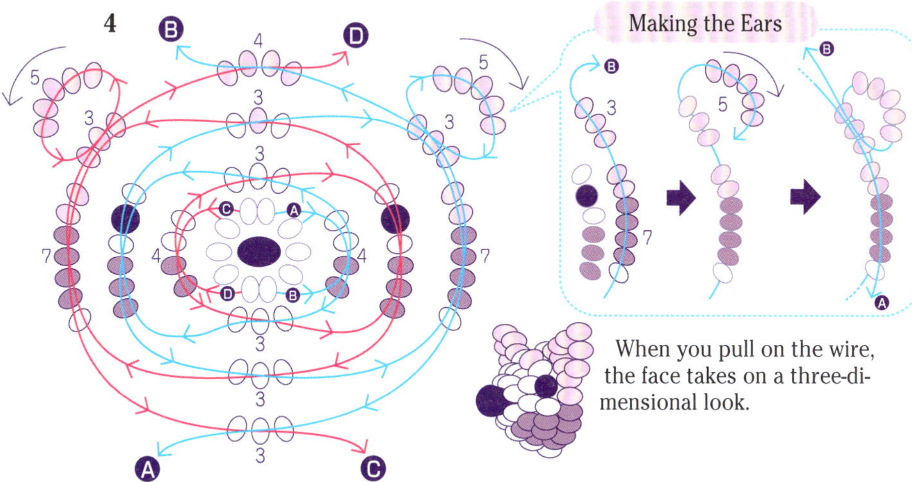

When you pull on the wire, the face takes on a three-dimensional look.

5. Turn piece over and make head. Twist A and B, and C and D wires together 3-4 times. Cut excess wire. After twisting the wire, fold ends under to prevent injury. Don't forget to string the split ring, because it won't open wide enough to allow you to add it later.

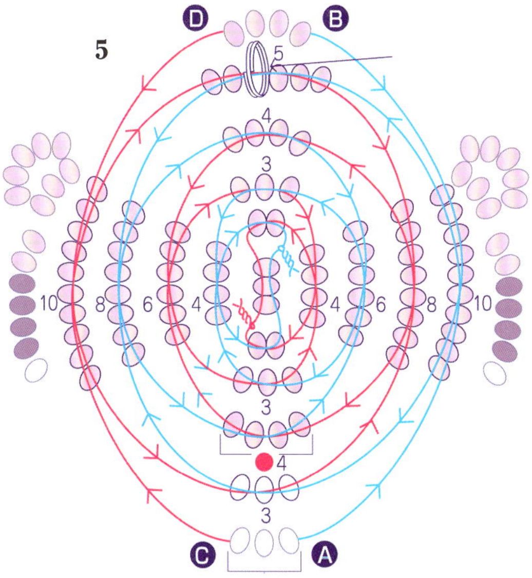

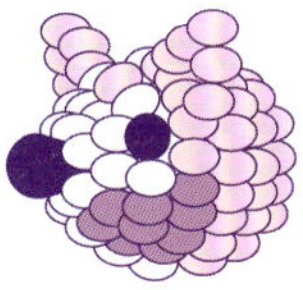

6. **Raccoon's body:** Cut two 40cm (16") lengths of wire. Pass them through beads (see diagram).

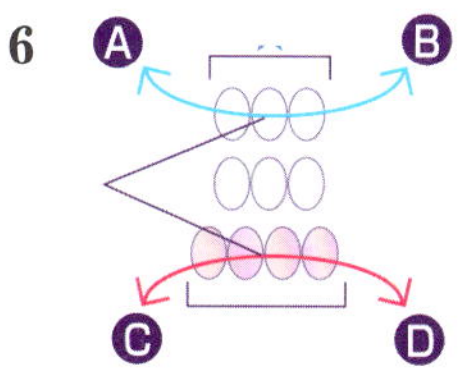

7. Add beads to make body and front legs.

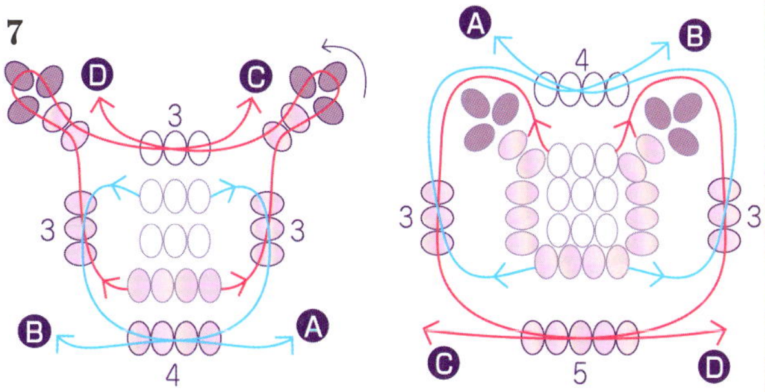

8. Make hind legs.

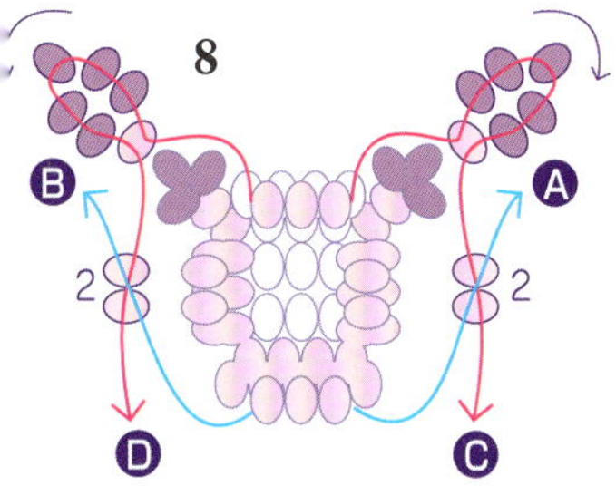

9. Make tail with C and D wires. Twist A and B, and C and D wires together 3-4 times. Cut excess wire. After twisting the wire, fold ends under to prevent injury.

10.

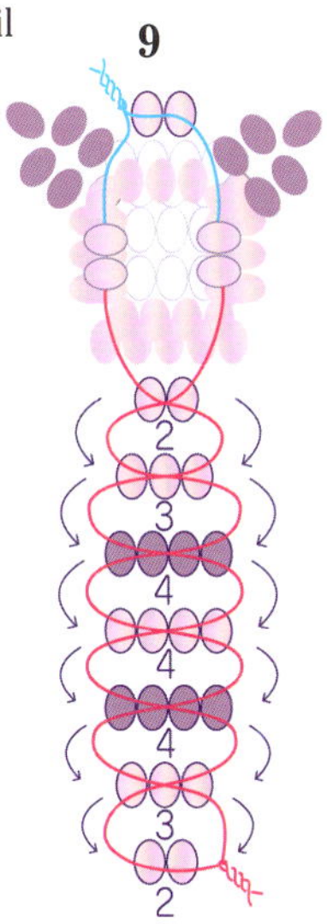

10. Adjust shape and insert key chain into split ring.

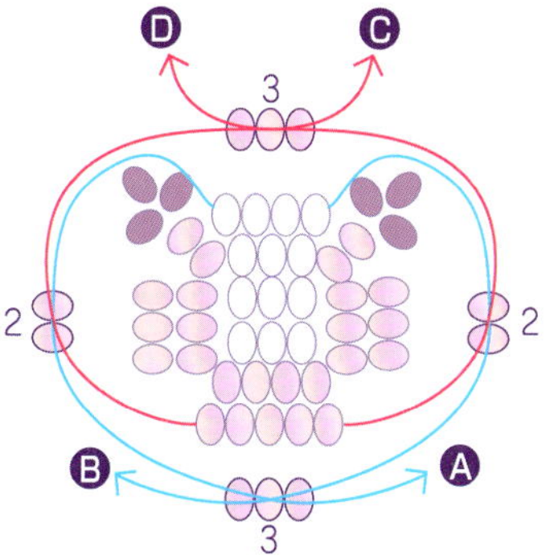

Bunny Blue never sparkled so much!

Worked in sky blue pastel and carrying his own carrot, this lop eared rabbit will hop right into your heart.

1. **Rabbit's head**: Tape 70cm (28") nylon thread down to work surface 8cm (3") away from end. Pass thread through 10mm acrylic bead.

1

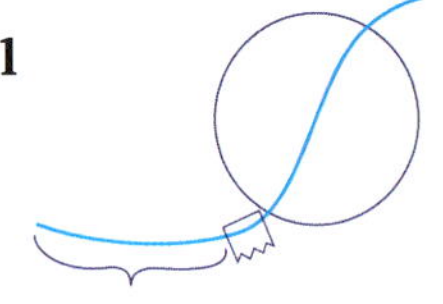

2. With taped end at the bottom, string beads on thread, wrapping them around 10mm bead.

2

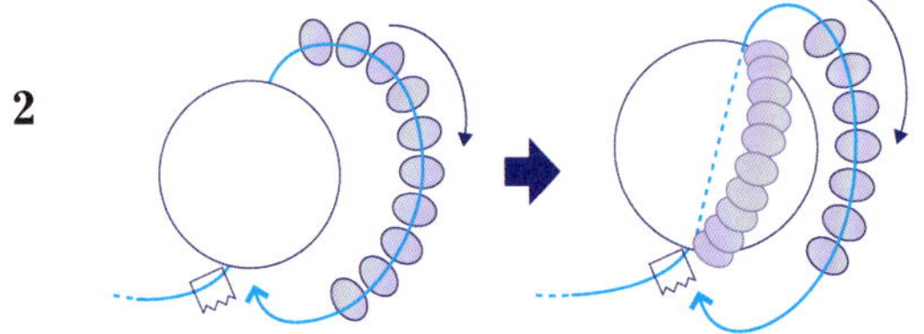

3. Continue stringing beads as in Step 2, paying careful attention to number and color. String beads in direction indicated by arrow in drawing. Shape head as you work.

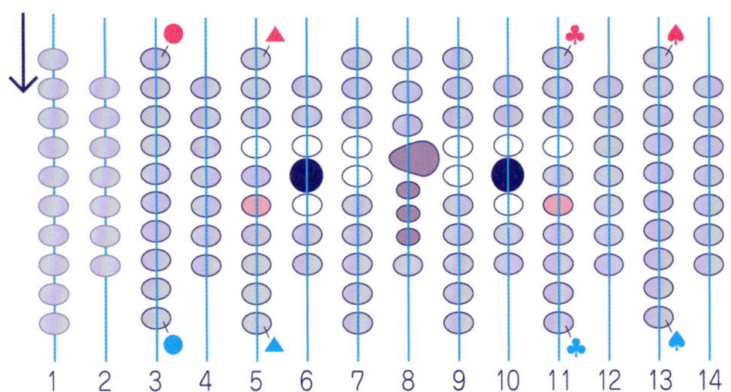

4

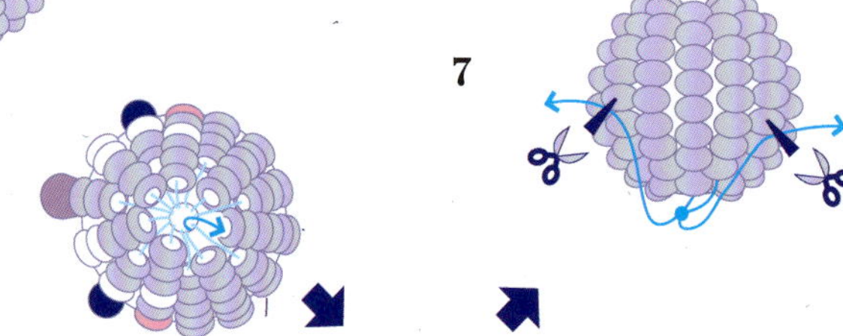

4. If a large area of the 10mm bead shows through after you've strung the beads for Row 14, add more rows until the bead is covered.

7

5

5. After you've strung the beads for the last row, pass thread through beads in Row 1.

6

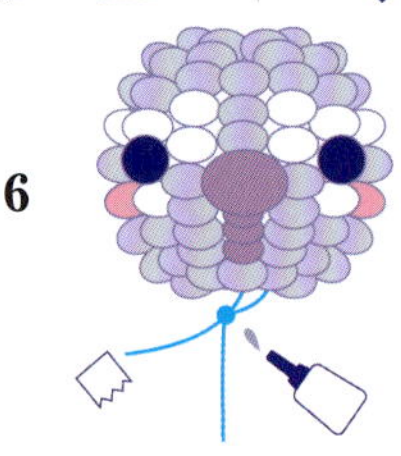

6. Remove tape at starting point. Tie threads together 2-3 times; apply glue sparingly to knot.

7. Run thread ends through 2-3 beads. Cut excess.

8. **Make ears and attach to head**: String beads on 30cm (12") wire.

8

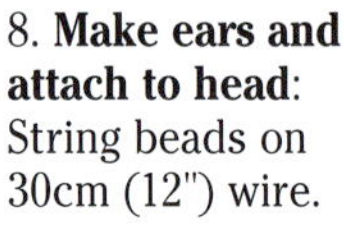

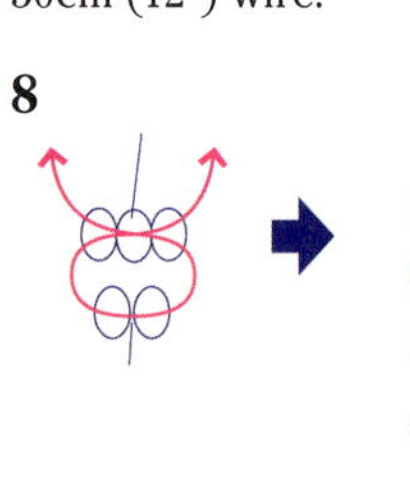

9. Pass wire through beads at top of Rows 3 and 5 of head. Then pass wire through acrylic bead (see diagram).

9

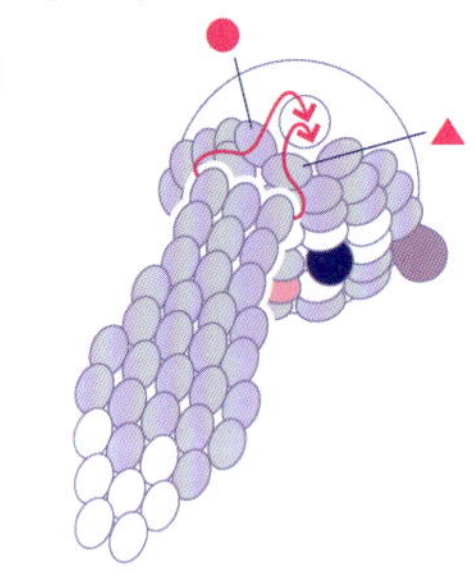

10. Pass wire through beads at bottom of Rows 3 and 5 (see diagram). Twist wires together and cut excess. After twisting the wire, fold ends under to prevent injury.

10

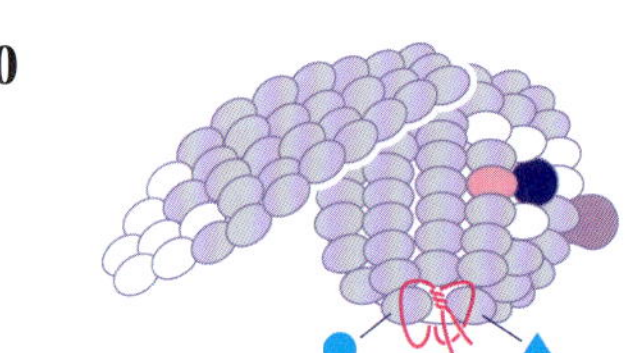

11. Repeat Steps 8-10 on opposite side of head, inserting wire into beads on Rows 11 and 13 to attach other ear.

11

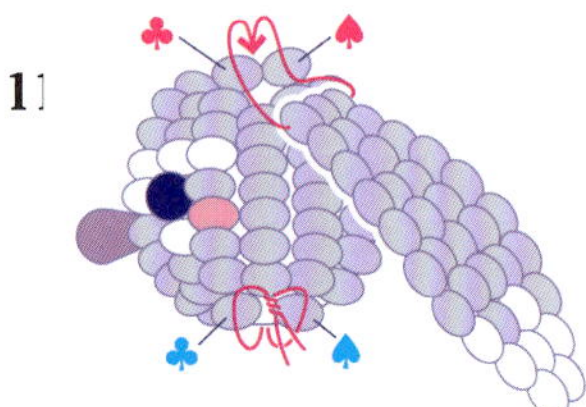

12. **Rabbit's body**: Use 50cm (20") nylon thread and 7mm acrylic bead. Follow directions for making head. After stringing beads for Row 12, finish as in Step 4.

12

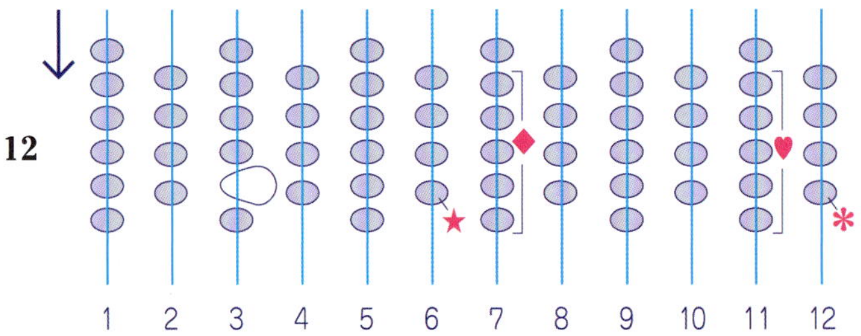

Materials:
Toho 11/0 seed beads (Pale Blue #146, White #777, Pink #970)
Toho 15/0 seed beads (Green #108, Brown #941)
Toho 4mm magatama beads (Brown #M46, White #M41)
7mm White acrylic bead with large hole
10mm White acrylic bead with large hole
Toho 3mm Black #PB-313 pop beads
Toho 2mm Orange #1105-2mm cat's-eye bead
Toho 3mm Orange #1105-3mm cat's-eye bead
Toho 4mm Orange #1104-4mm cat's-eye bead
32 Gauge silver wire • Split ring • Head pin • Key chain • #2 nylon thread

13. **Carrot**: String beads on 30cm (12") wire. Twist wire together with end left at starting point 3-4 times; cut excess wire. After twisting wire, fold ends under to prevent injury.

13

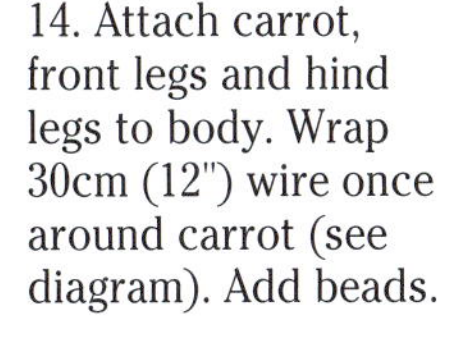

14. Attach carrot, front legs and hind legs to body. Wrap 30cm (12") wire once around carrot (see diagram). Add beads.

14

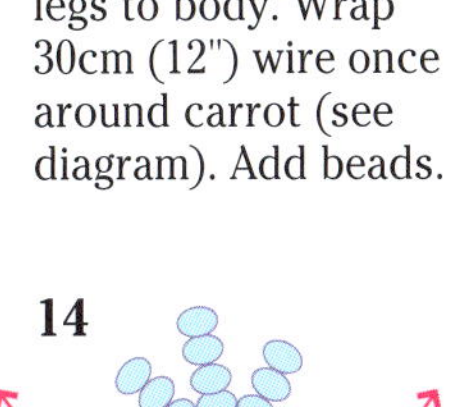

15. Pass wire through 5 beads in Row 7 of body. On opposite side, pass wire through beads in Row 11 (see diagram).

15

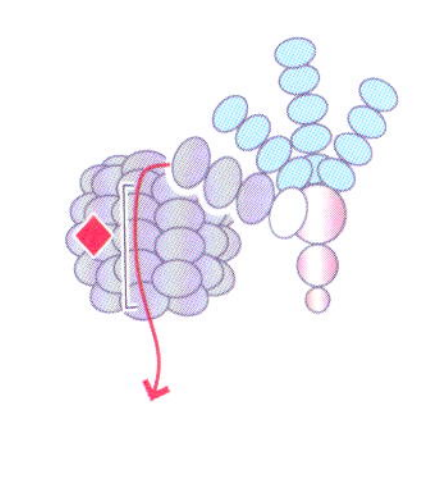

16. String beads to make hind leg, referring to diagram. Pass wire through bead at bottom of Row 6.

16

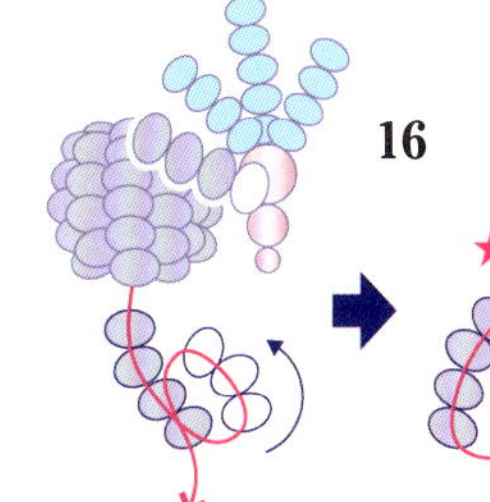

17. On opposite side, string beads in the same way. Pass wire through bead at bottom of Row 12 (see diagram).

17

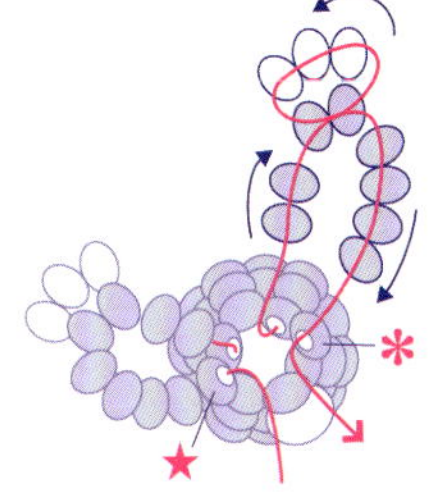

18. Twist the two wires together. Cut excess wire. After twisting the wire, fold ends under to prevent injury.

18

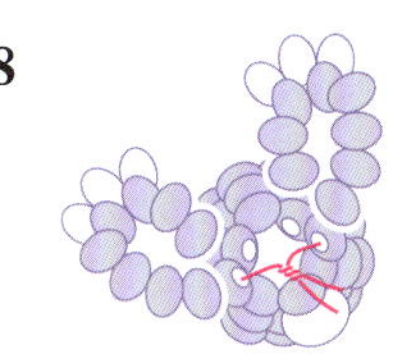

19. Attach key chain. Cut shaft of head pin to 3cm (1 1/4"). Insert head pin into body and head, in that order. Round end of head pin. See page 2 instructions Using Head Pins.

19

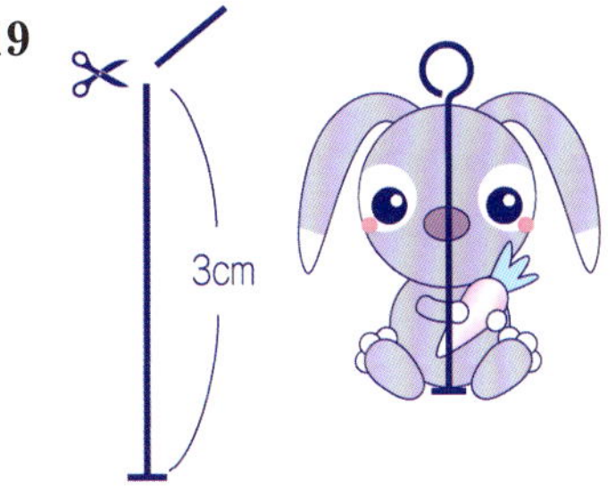

20. Insert head pin into split ring. Insert key chain into split ring. See page 2 instructions Adding a Split Ring.

20

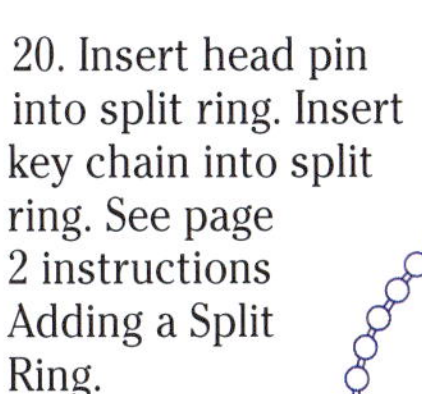

Just a spring chick!

This cute yellow friend makes everybody smile.

Materials:
Toho 11/0 seed beads (Yellow #102, Orange #957)
7mm White acrylic bead with large hole
10mm White acrylic bead with large hole
Toho 3mm Black #PB–313 pop beads
32 Gauge gold wire • Split ring • Head pin • Key chain • Nylon thread

1. **Chick's head**: Tape 70cm (28") nylon thread down to work surface 8cm (3") away from end. Pass other end of thread through 10mm acrylic bead.

1

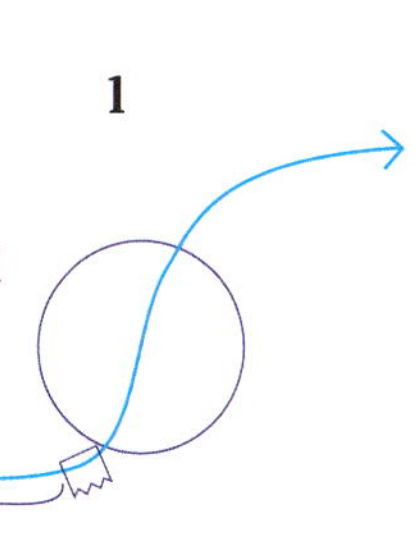

2. With taped end at the bottom, string beads on thread, wrapping them around 10mm bead.

2

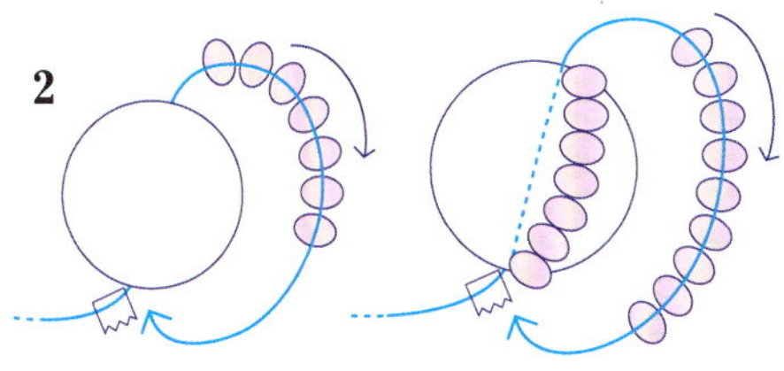

instructions continued on page 10

instructions continued from page 9

3. Continue stringing beads as in Step 2, paying careful attention to number and color. Once you've strung beads for Row 9, go back to Row 6 to make beak, referring to Making the beak. Once you've strung beads for Row 9, run thread through beads in Row 6. Shape face as you work.

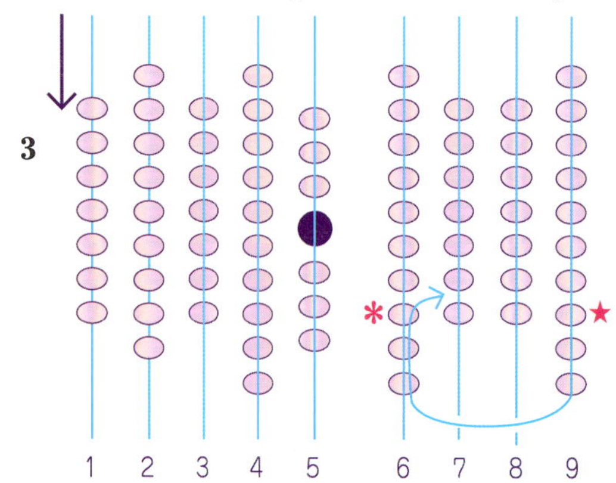

4. **Making the Beak:** Once you've strung beads for Row 9, go back to Row 6 to make beak, referring to Making the beak. Once you've strung beads for Row 9, run thread through beads in Row 6. Shape face as you work.

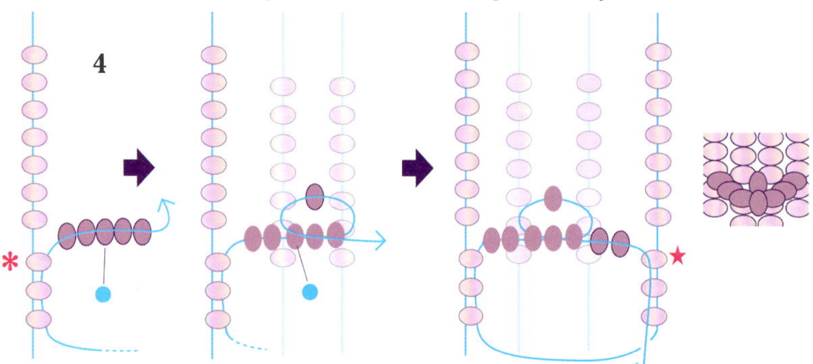

5. If a large area of the 10mm bead shows through after you've strung the beads for Row 15, add more rows until the bead is covered.

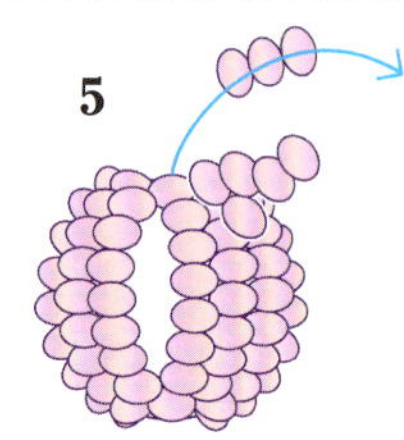

6. After you've strung the beads for the last row, run thread through beads on Row 1. Tie thread to end left at starting point 2-3 times.

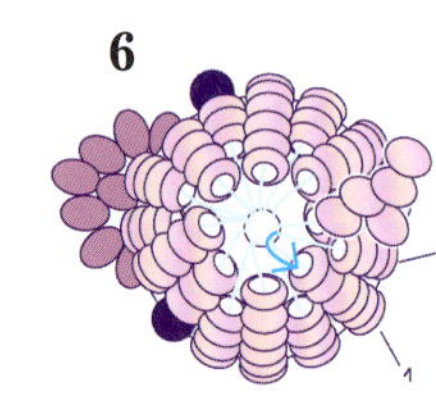

7. Remove tape. Apply glue sparingly to knot.

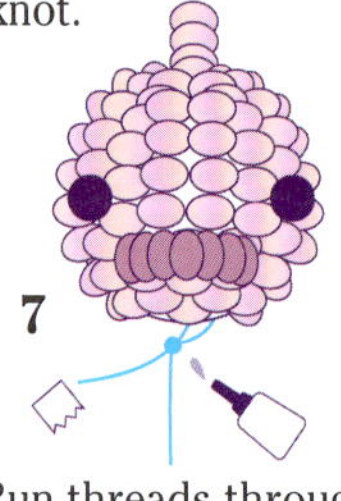

8. Run threads through 2-3 beads; cut excess.

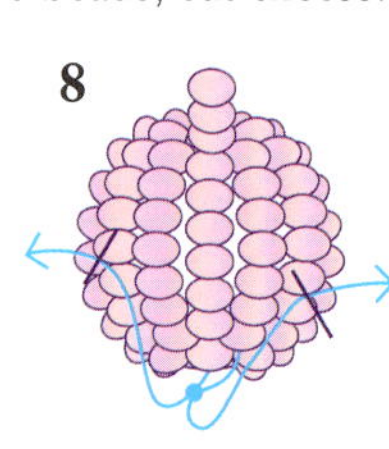

9. **Chick's body**: Use the 7mm acrylic bead and 50cm (20") nylon thread. The body is made in the same way as the head. After stringing beads for Row 11, finish in same way as Step 6.

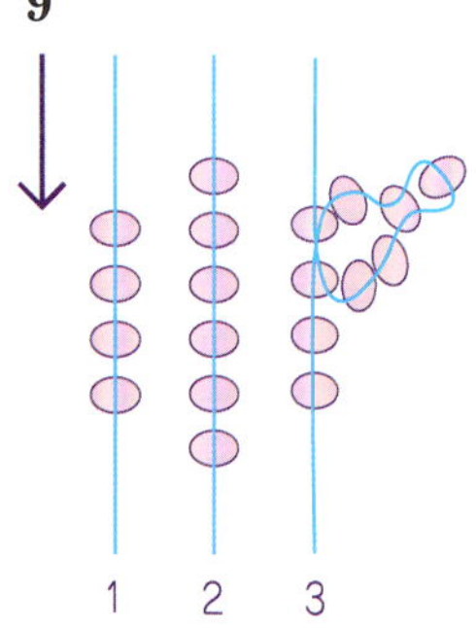
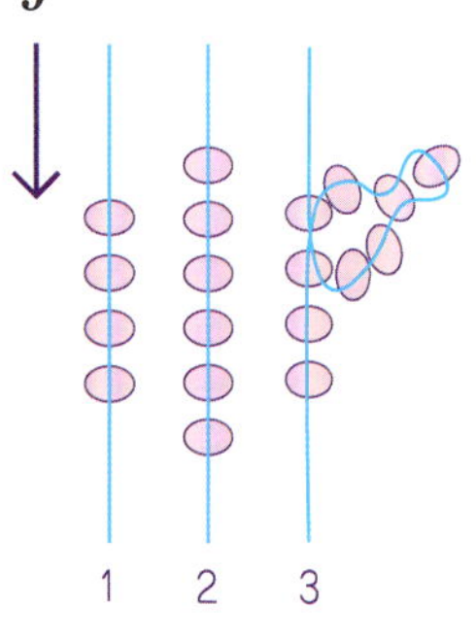

Making the wings:

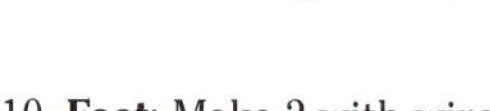

10. **Feet**: Make 2 with wire.

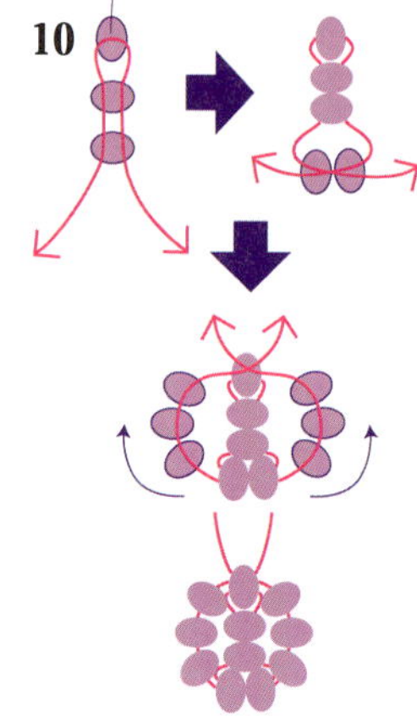

11. Attach feet where indicated in diagrams. Pass wire through beads as shown.

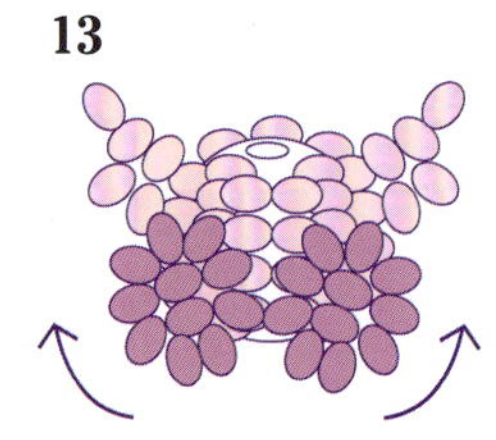

12. Twist wires together 2-3 times. Cut excess.

13. Bend feet upwards. After twisting the wire, fold ends under to prevent injury.

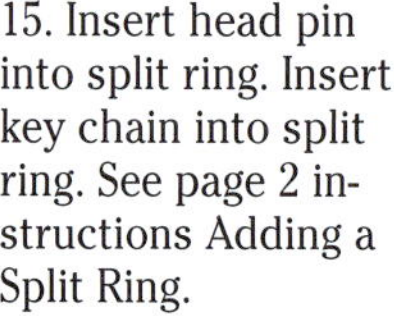

14. Attach key chain: Cut shaft of head pin to 3cm (1¼"). Pass head pin through body, then head, in that order. Round end of head pin. See page 2 instructions Using Head Pins.

15. Insert head pin into split ring. Insert key chain into split ring. See page 2 instructions Adding a Split Ring.

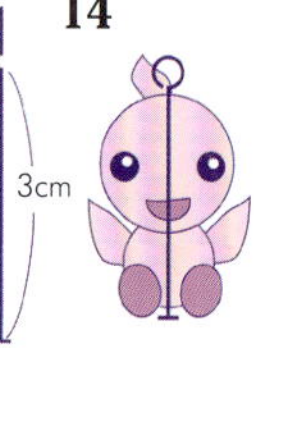

Materials:

Toho 11/0 seed beads (White #41, Black #49, Green #108, Blue #933)
Toho 4mm Black #M49 magatama bead
7mm White acrylic bead with large hole
10mm White acrylic bead with large hole
Toho 3mm Black #PB-313 pop beads
Split ring • Head pins • Key chain • Nylon thread

1. **Koala's head:** Tape 70cm (28") nylon of thread to work surface 8cm (3") away from the end. Pass thread through a 10mm White acrylic bead.

2. With taped end at the bottom, string beads on thread. Wrap them around the 10mm bead.

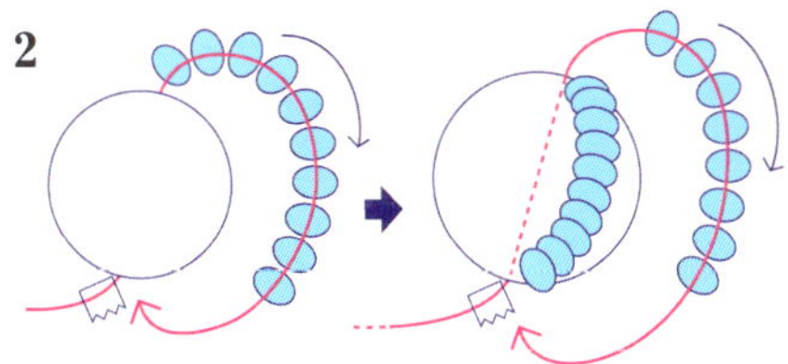

3. Continue stringing beads as in Step 2, paying careful attention to number and color. String beads in direction indicated by arrows.

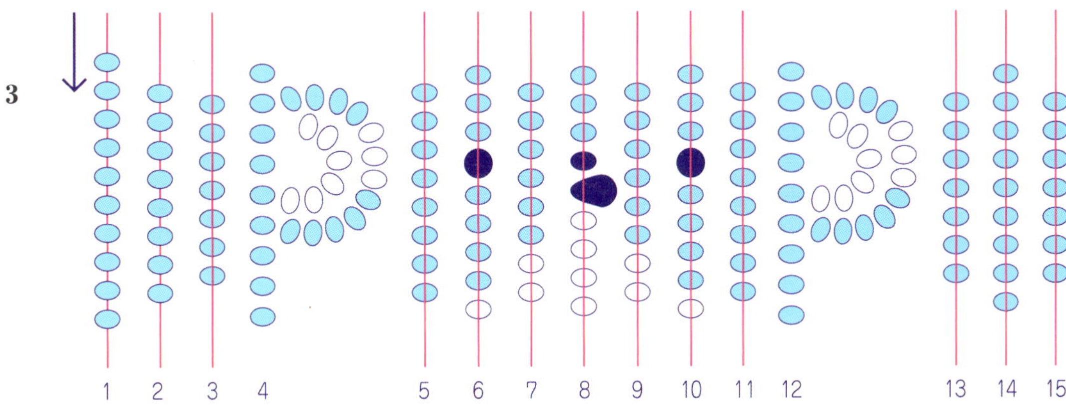

4. **Making the Ears:** Pull thread as you work so there is no slack.

5. If a large area of the 10mm bead shows through after you've strung the beads for Row 15, add more rows until the bead is covered. After you've strung the beads for the last row, pass thread through beads in Row 1. Tie thread to end left at starting point 2-3 times.

6. Remove tape; apply glue (sparingly) to knot.

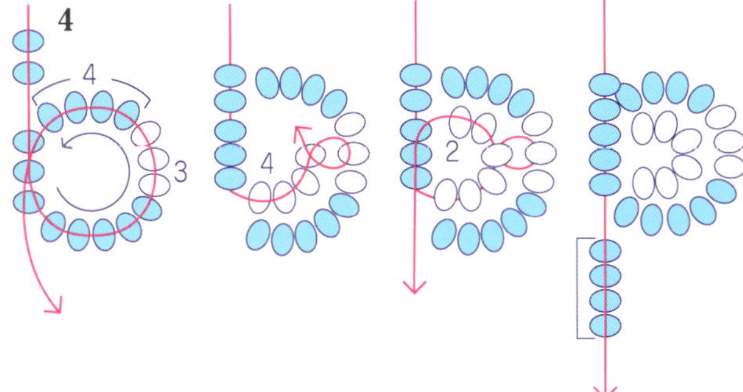

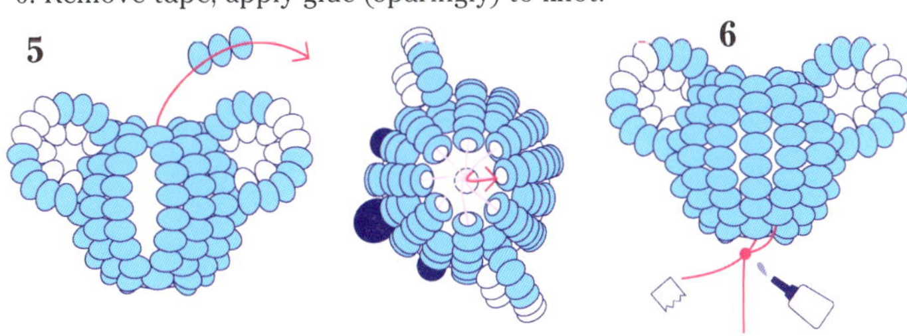

7. Run threads through 2-3 beads; cut excess.

8. **Koala's body:** Use the 7mm acrylic bead and 60cm (24") nylon thread. The body is made in the same way as the head. After stringing beads for Row 11, finish in same way as Step 5.

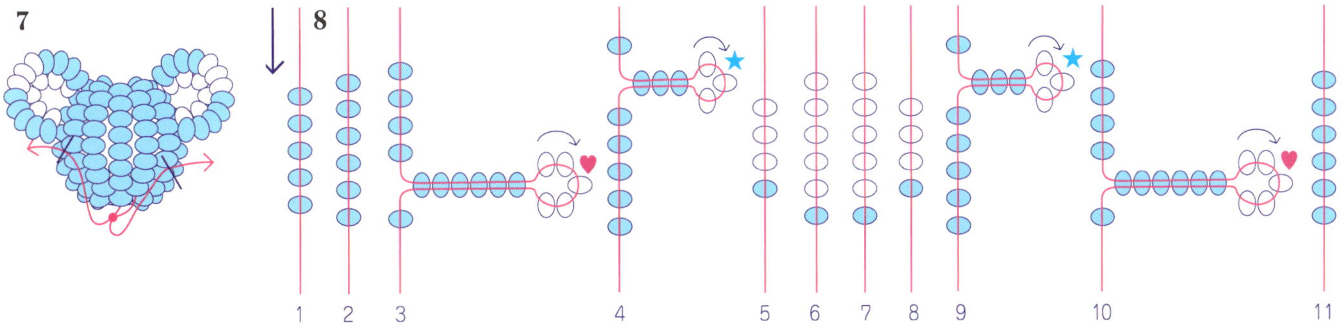

instructions continued on page 10

instructions continued from page 9

Koala bears survive primarily on eucalyptus leaves and spend 75% of their time sleeping in the branches of trees. It must be dusk, for this little guy is wide awake grasping his favorite food.

9. Make the branch and attach to arm and leg: String beads on 50cm (20") thread.

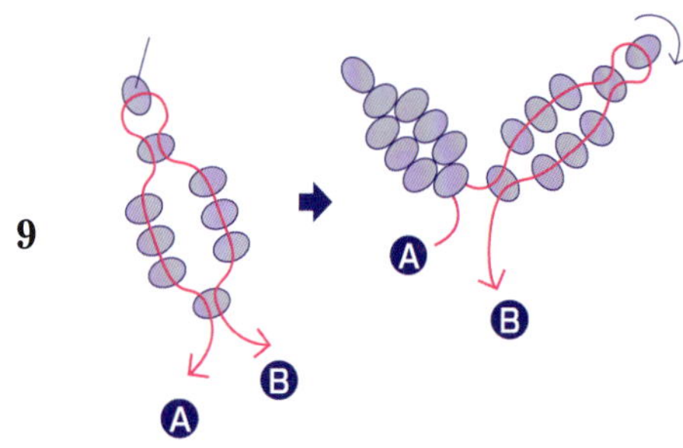

10. String Green seed beads for branch, positioning it in front of koala's stomach. Add Green seed beads, passing thread through beads for arm and leg (see diagram). Tie threads together and cut excess. Apply glue to knot.

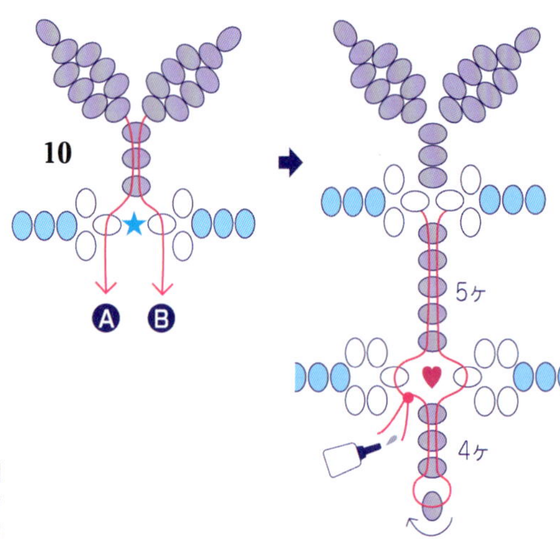

11. M body the r when you attach the branch.

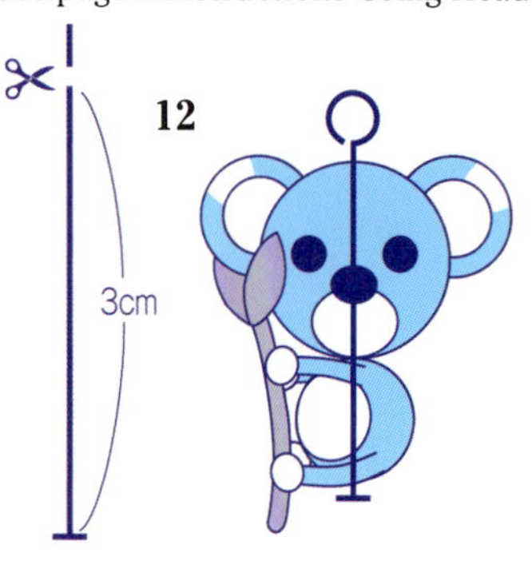

12. **Attach key chain**: Cut shaft of head pin to 3cm (1¼"). Pass head pin through body and head. Round end of head pin. See page 2 instructions Using Head Pins.

13. Attach split ring to head pin. Insert key chain into split ring. Close key chain. See page 2 instructions Adding a Split Ring.

Materials:
Toho 11/0 seed beads (White #41, Pink #910, Blue #932, Yellow #949)
Toho 3mm Black #PB-313 pop beads
7mm White acrylic bead with large hole
10mm White acrylic bead with large hole
Split ring • Head pin • Wire • Key chain • Nylon thread

1. **Penguin's head**: Tape 70cm (28") nylon thread down to work surface 8cm (3") away from end. Pass thread through 10mm acrylic bead.

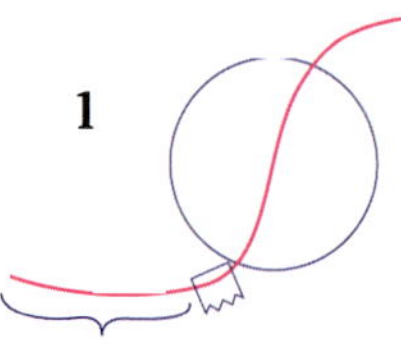

2. With taped end at the bottom, string beads on thread, wrapping them around 10mm bead.

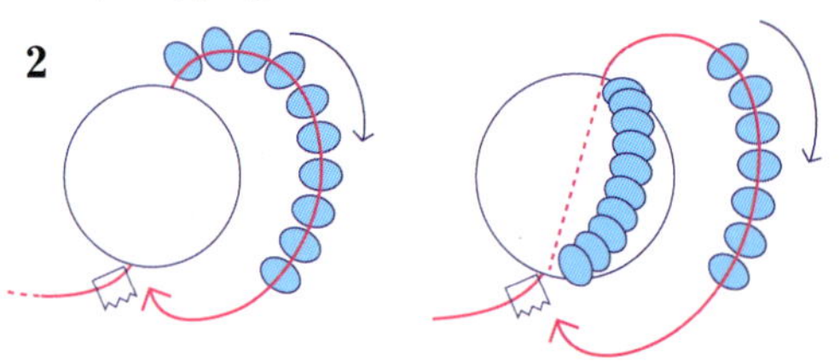

3. Continue stringing beads as in Step 2, paying careful attention to number and color. String beads in direction indicated by arrows. After stringing beads for Row 10, go back to Row 8 and through last 3 beads. String on 6 beads for beak. Go back through last 3 beads of Row 10 (see diagram).

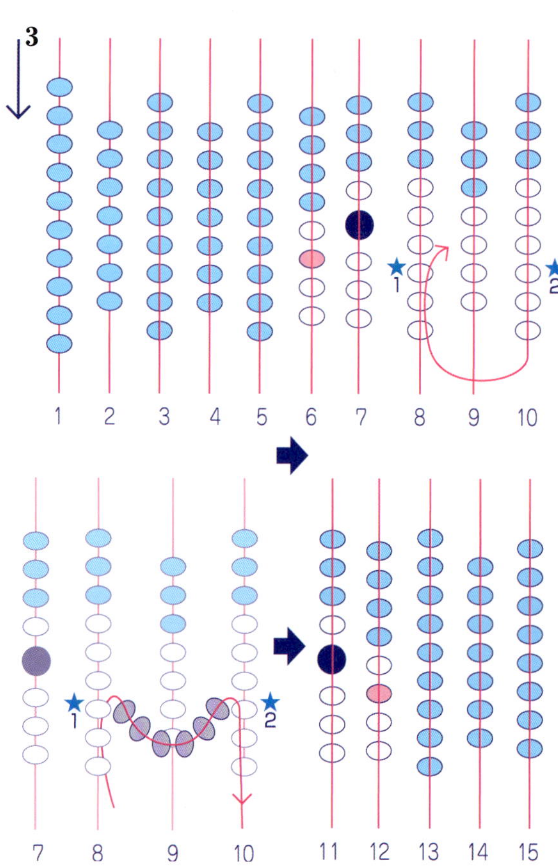

Having discarded the traditional tuxedo look, our well dressed penguin sports plumage in crisp blue and white.

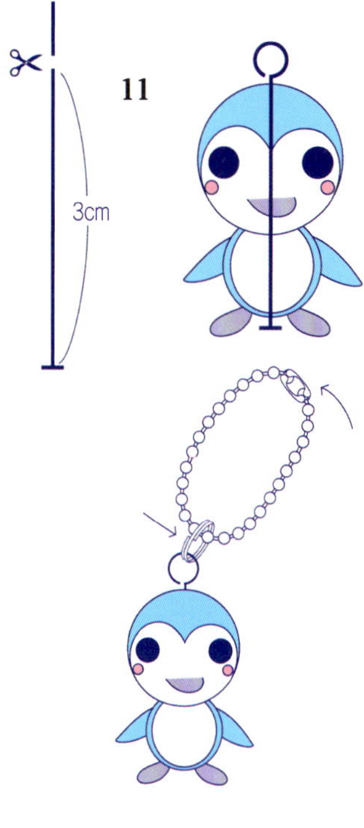

4. If a large area of the 10mm bead shows through after you've strung the beads for Row 15, add more rows until the bead is covered. After stringing beads for the last row, run thread through the beads on Row 1. Tie thread to end left at starting point 2-3 times.

4

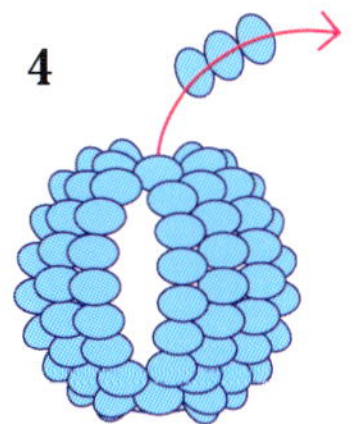

5. Remove tape; apply glue sparingly to knot.

6. Run thread through 2-3 beads; cut excess.

5

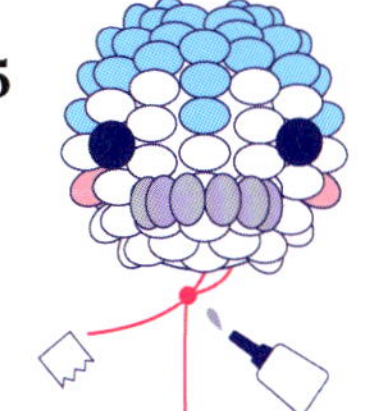

6

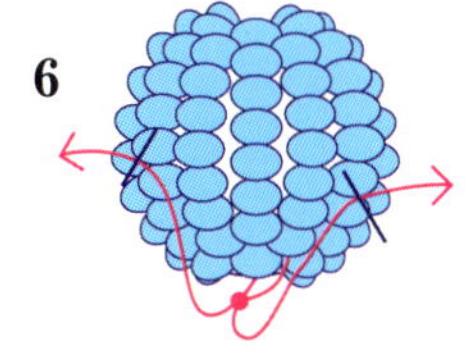

11. Attach split ring to headpin. Insert key chain into split ring. Close key chain. See page 2 instructions Adding a Split Ring.

11

7. **Penguin's body**: Use the 7mm acrylic bead and 50cm (20") nylon thread. The body is made in the same way as the head. After stringing the beads for Row 12, go back to Row 4 and make the feet and tail.

7

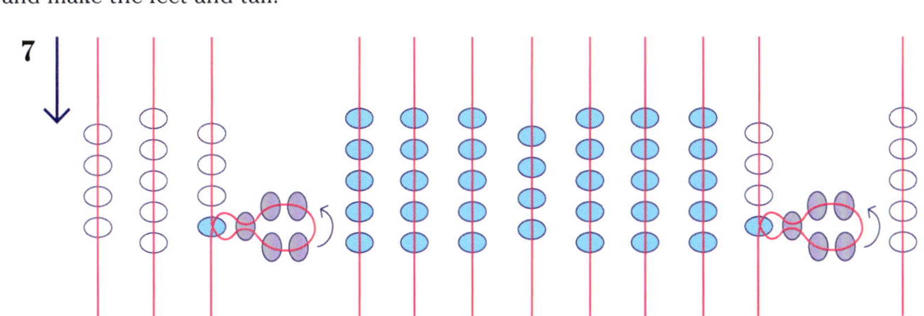

8. **Making the feet:**

9. **Making the wings and tail:**

8

9

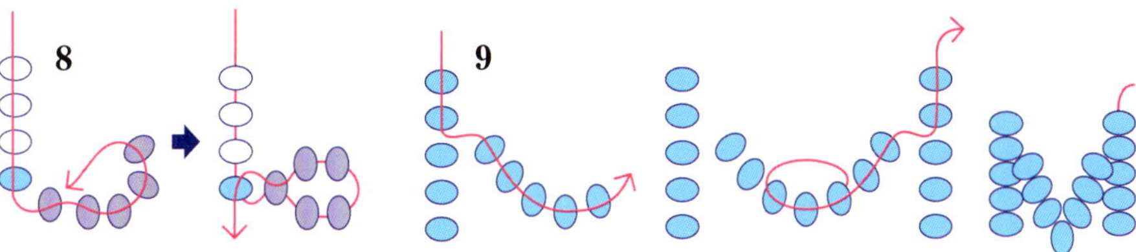

10. After stringing beads for Row 11, finish in same way as Step 4. Tie thread to end left at starting point.

10

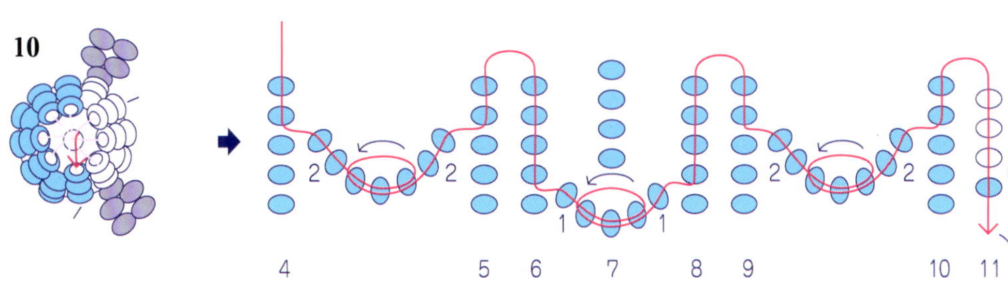

Materials:
Toho 11/0 seed beads (Red #5, Orange #30, White #41,
    Yellow #42, Black #49, Pink #906)
Toho 4mm Red #M05 magatama bead
5mm White acrylic bead with large hole
7mm White acrylic bead with large hole
10mm White acrylic bead with large hole
Toho 3mm Black #PB-313 pop beads
32 Gauge gold wire • Head pin • Split ring • Key chain • #2 nylon
    thread

Teaching a baby chick to fly or just stay out of trouble is a lot of work, but beading this charming pair is a lot of fun.

Gather your beads and supplies and begin making your Beaded Mini Menagerie today!

1 1. **Rooster's head**: Tape 75cm (30") nylon thread down to work surface 8cm (3") away from end. Pass thread through 10mm acrylic bead.

2. With taped end at the bottom, string beads on thread, wrapping them around 10mm bead.

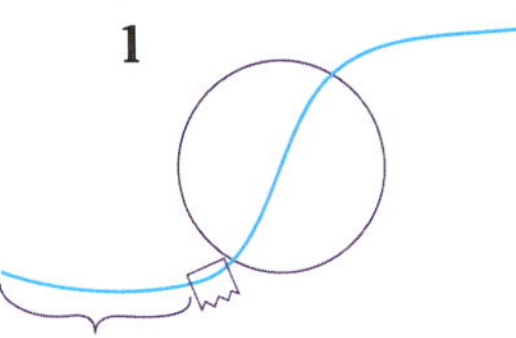

2

3. Continue stringing beads as in Step 2, paying careful attention to number and color. After you've strung the beads for Row 9, run thread through beads in Row 7 to make the beak (see diagram).

3

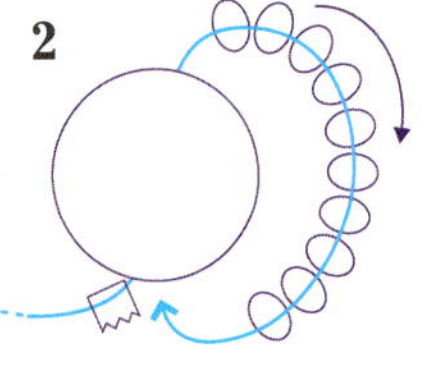
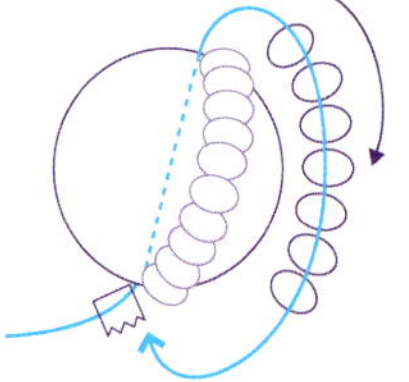

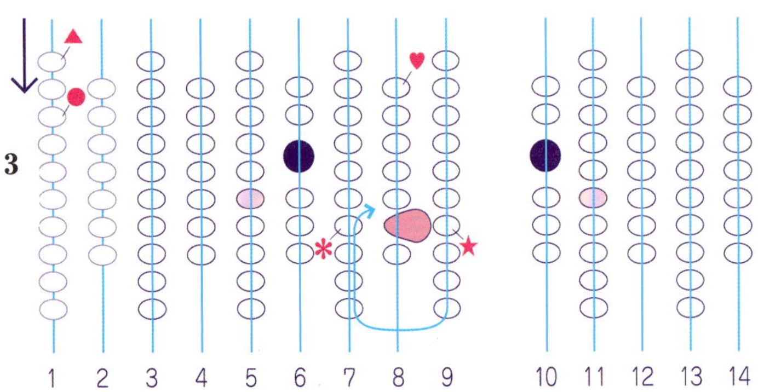

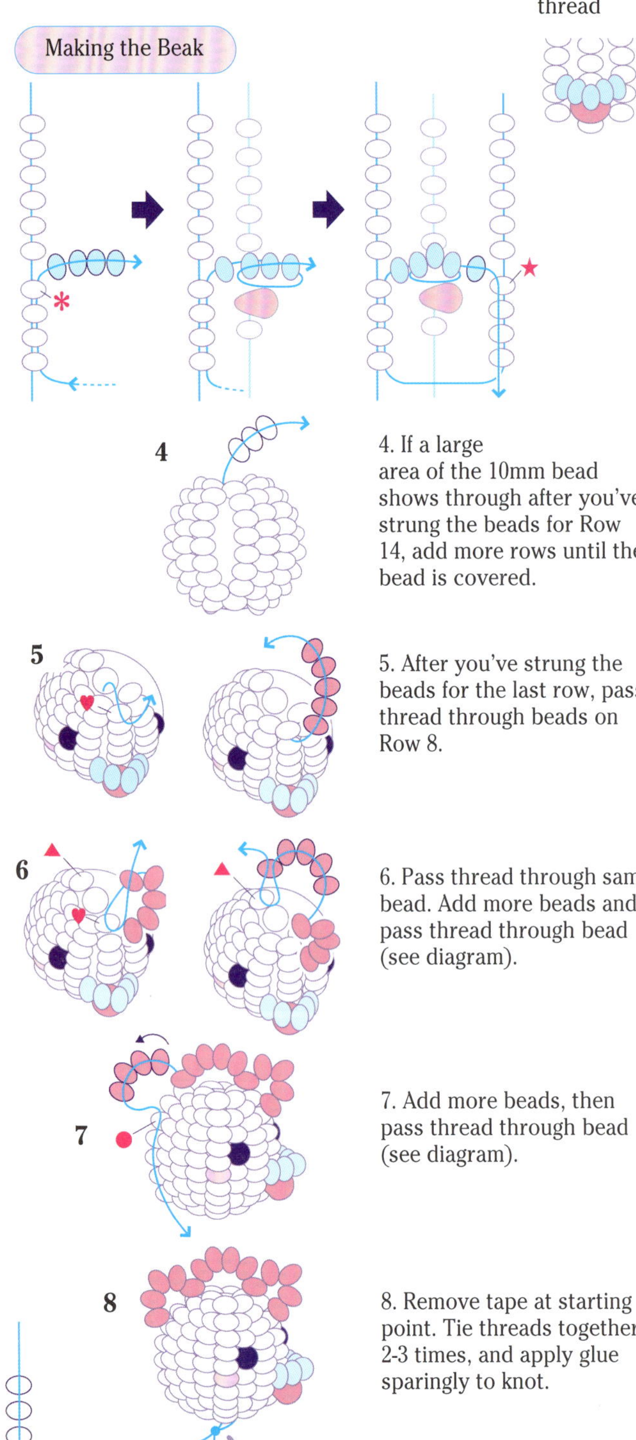

Making the Beak

4. If a large area of the 10mm bead shows through after you've strung the beads for Row 14, add more rows until the bead is covered.

4

5. After you've strung the beads for the last row, pass thread through beads on Row 8.

5

6. Pass thread through same bead. Add more beads and pass thread through bead (see diagram).

6

7. Add more beads, then pass thread through bead (see diagram).

7

8. Remove tape at starting point. Tie threads together 2-3 times, and apply glue sparingly to knot.

8

9. Run thread ends through 2-3 beads. Cut excess thread.

9

10. **Rooster's body**: Use the 7mm acrylic bead and 55cm (22") nylon thread. The body is made in the same way as the head.

Making the Tail

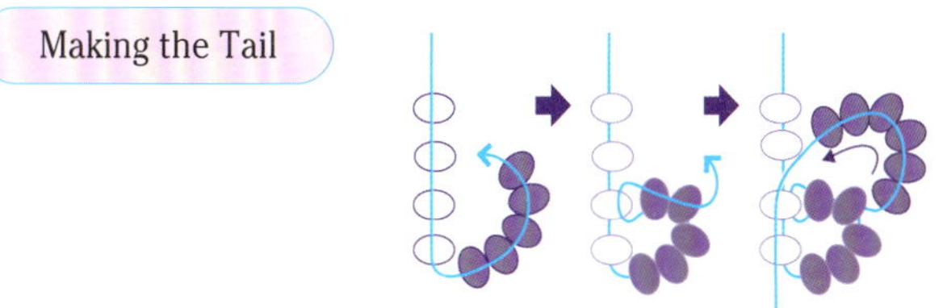

11. After stringing beads for Row 11, pass thread through beads in Row 1. Finish in same way as Step 7.

11

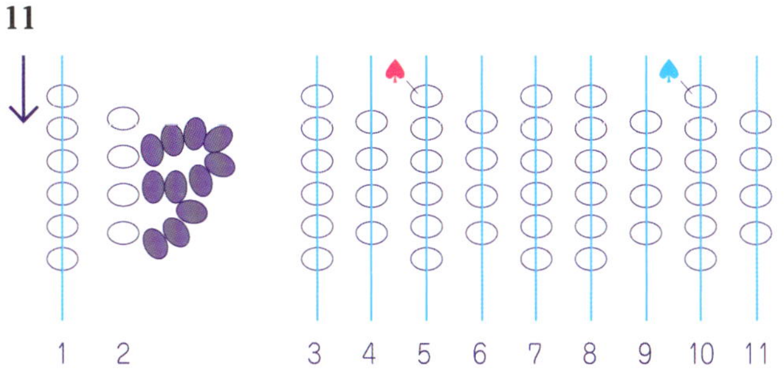

12. **Chick**: Use the 5mm acrylic bead and 50cm (20") thread. Chick is made in same way as rooster's head. After stringing beads for Row 11, pass thread through beads (see diagram). Finish in same way as Step 8.

12

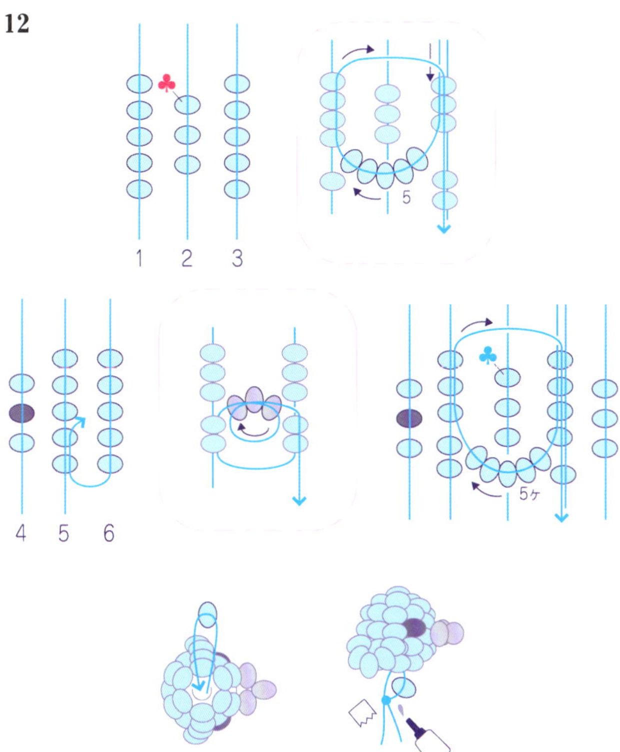

13. **Rooster's wings and legs**: Cut two 25cm (10") lengths of wire. String beads on one length to make foot, referring to diagrams.

13

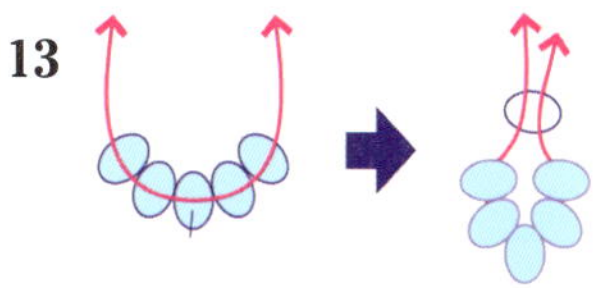

14

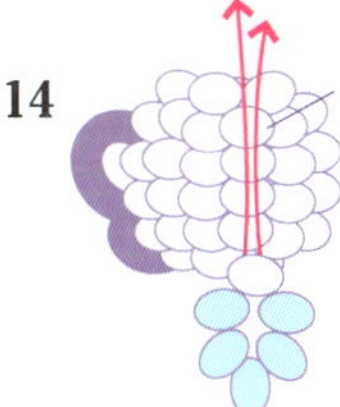

14. Pass wire through beads in Row 6 of body made in Step 10.

15. Pass other length of wire through bead in Row 5. Make wing and attach it to chick. Pass thread through top 3 beads in Row 5 (see diagram). Twist wire together 3-4 times; cut excess.

15

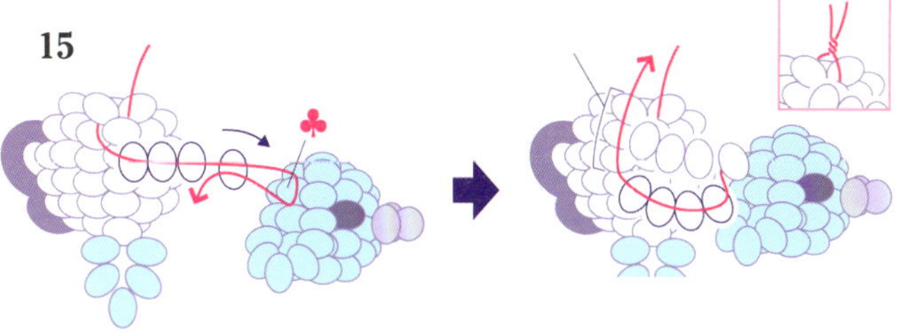

16. Make second wing with other length of wire. Pass wire through top 3 beads in Row 10. After twisting the wire, fold ends under to prevent injury.

16

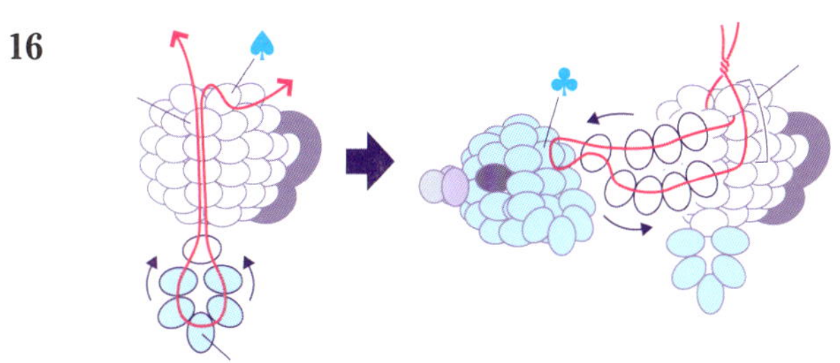

17. Attach key chain. Cut shaft of head pin to 3cm (1¹/₄"). Insert head pin into body and head, in that order. Round end of head pin. Attach Split ring to rooster's cocks comb and rounded end of head pin. See page 2 instructions Using Head Pins and Working with Split ring.

17

18. Insert key chain into Split ring.

18

This panda steps to his own beat. Join the fun and take a stand for individuality with this unique beaded musician.

1. **Panda's face**: Cut two 50cm (20") lengths of wire. String beads on one length wire.

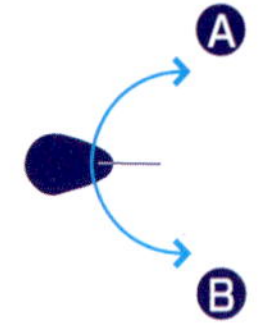

2. Form an intersection with wire in White seed beads.

3. String beads on other length wire, referring to diagram.

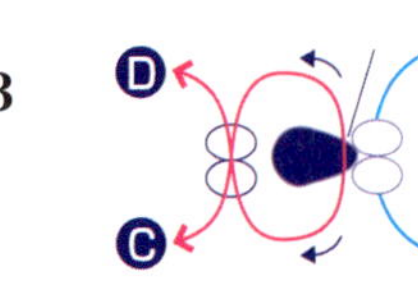

4. Add more beads forming intersections as you go.

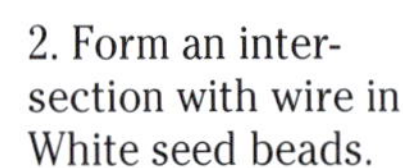

5. Complete the face. Pull wire so that first bead strung (magatama bead) rises above the plane of the other beads.

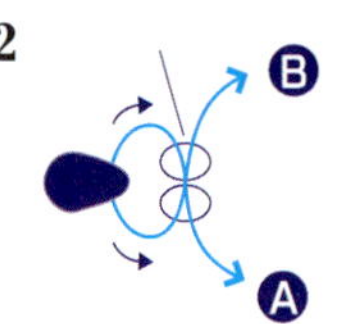

6. **Make ears.**

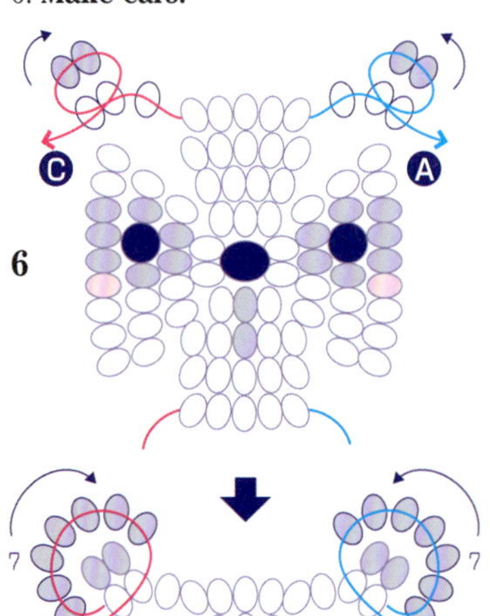

7. Turn piece over and make back of head. Twist A and B, and C and D wires together 3-4 times. Cut excess wire. After twisting the wire, fold ends under to prevent injury.

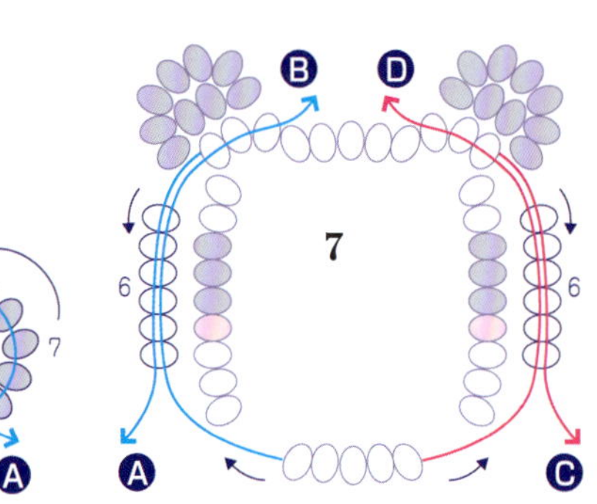

8. Add split ring here, because it won't open wide enough to allow you to add it later.

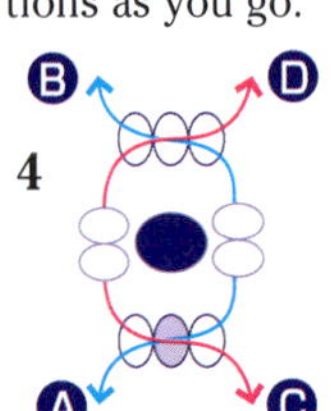

9. **Panda's body**: Cut two 50cm (20") lengths of wire. Pass wires through beads in head (see diagram).

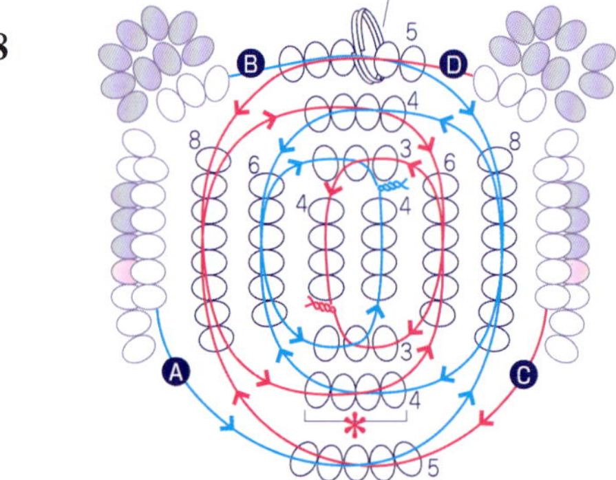

10. C

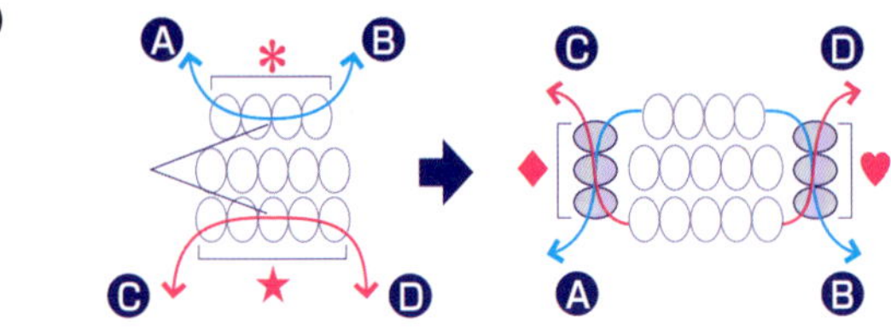

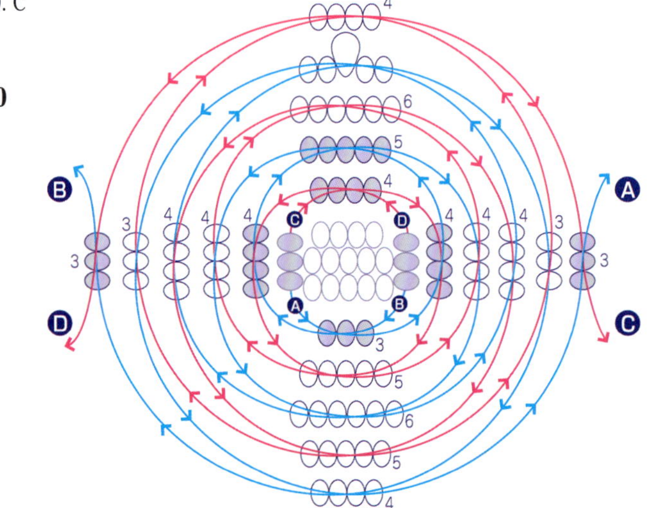

Materials:
Toho 11/0 seed beads (White #41, Black #49, Pink #908)
Toho 8/0 Orange #111 seed beads
Toho 6mm Pale Blue #146 bugle beads
Toho 4mm magatama beads (Black #M49, White #M41)
Toho 3mm Black #PB-313 pop beads
Toho Pink #PB-781 bead
32 Gauge silver wire • Split ring • Key chain

11. Make hind legs. Twist A and C, and B and D wires together 3-4 times. Cut excess wire. After twisting the wire, fold ends under to prevent injury.

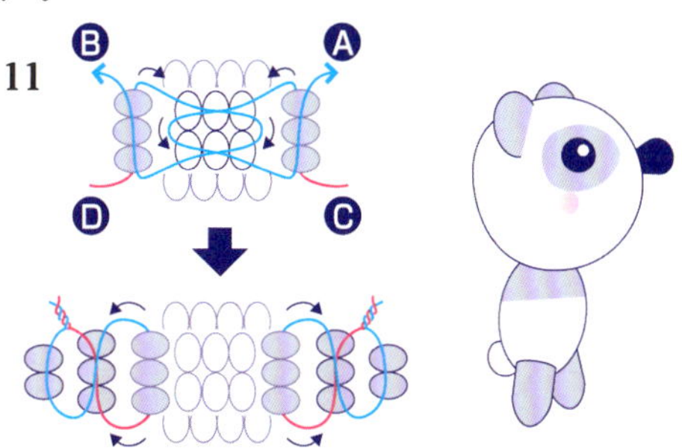

12. **Front legs and drum**: Pass 30cm (12") wire through beads (see diagram). Form intersections in beads as shown in drawings.

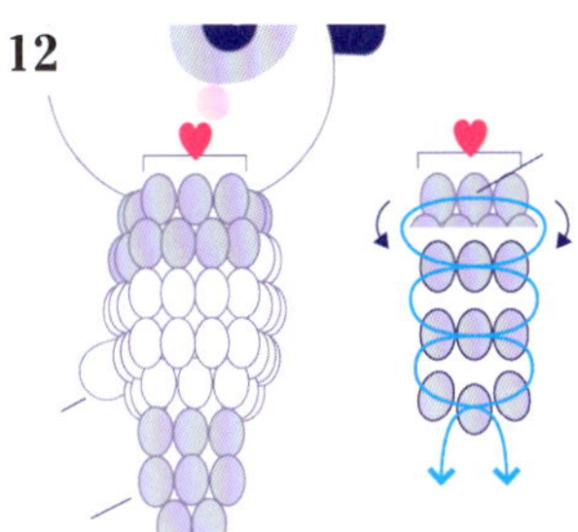

13. String bugle beads, 8/0 seed beads, novelty beads and 11/0 seed beads on wire to make drum.

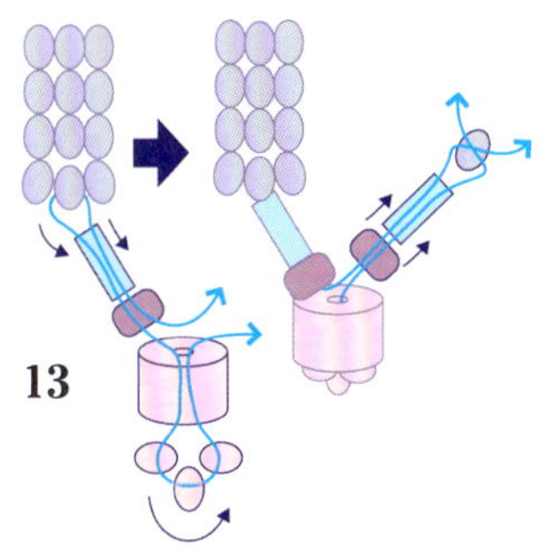

14. Make other front leg. Pass wire through beads. Twist wires together 3-4 times. Cut excess wire. After twisting the wire, fold ends under to prevent injury.

15. Adjust shape of panda. Insert key chain into split ring.

Here kitty, kitty. A must-have beaded critter for every cat lover, ours even brings her own bell.

Materials:
Toho 11/0 seed beads (White #41, Gray #282, Brown #951, Red #341)
Toho 8/0 White #122 seed beads
Toho 4mm Black #M49 magatama bead
Toho Black # PB-313 pop beads
#34 Gold wire • 10cm Black cord • Split ring
• Crimp beads • Bell • Key chain

1. **Cat's whiskers**: Cut cord in half. Leaving a 2cm end, string beads and crimp beads onto cord. Compress crimp bead with pliers.

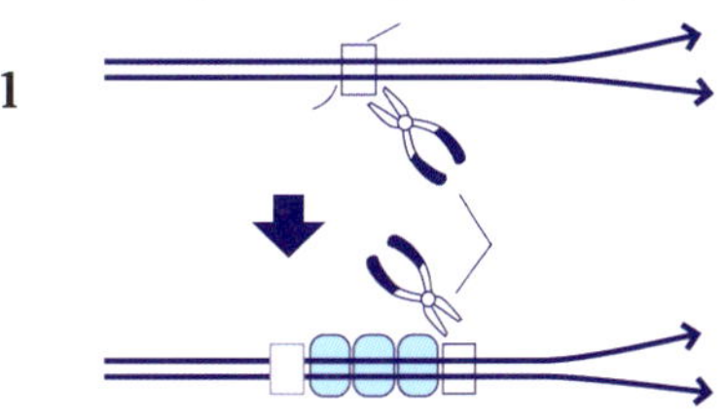

2. **Cat's face**: Cut two 50cm (20") lengths of wire. String magatama bead on one length of wire.

3. Form an intersection in White 11/0 seed beads with wire.

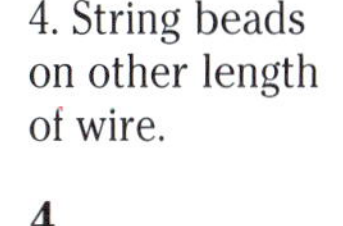

4. String beads on other length of wire.

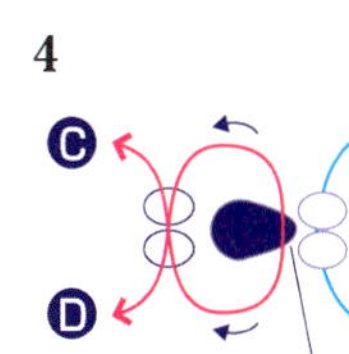

5. Add more beads, forming intersections as you go.

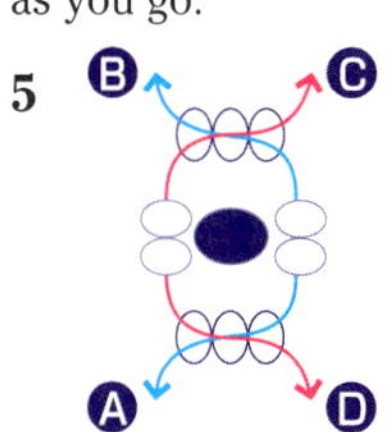

6. Complete the face. Add split ring here because it won't open wide enough to allow you to add it later. Pull wire so that first bead strung (magatama bead) rises above the plane of the other beads.

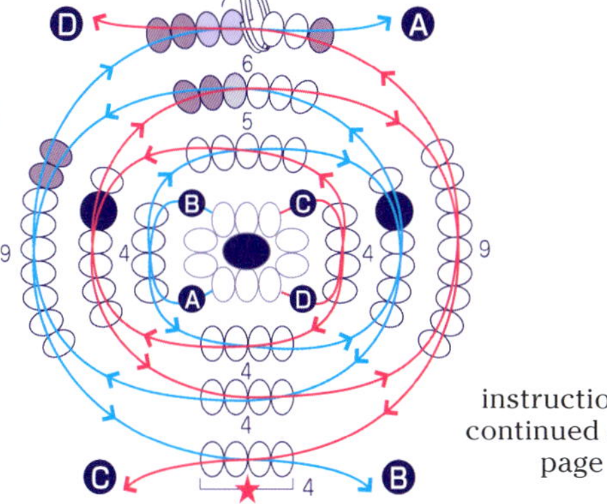

instructions continued on page 16

Calico Cat instructions continued from page 15

7. Position of whiskers (see diagram).

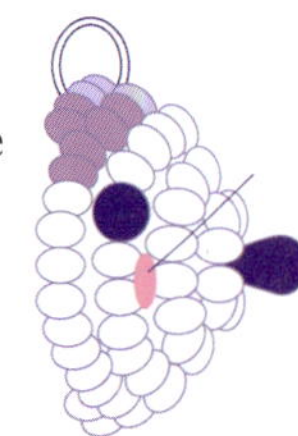

7

8. Insert whiskers from behind.

9. Cut whiskers to the length that you prefer.

8
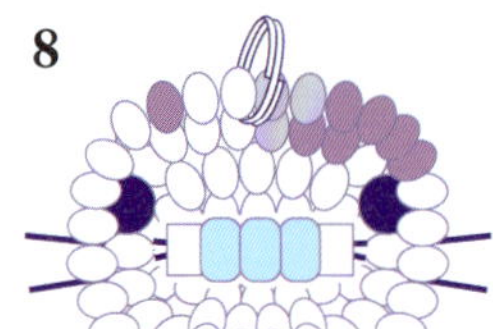

9

10. **Ears**: String beads on wire, working toward back of piece. Make other ear in same way.

10
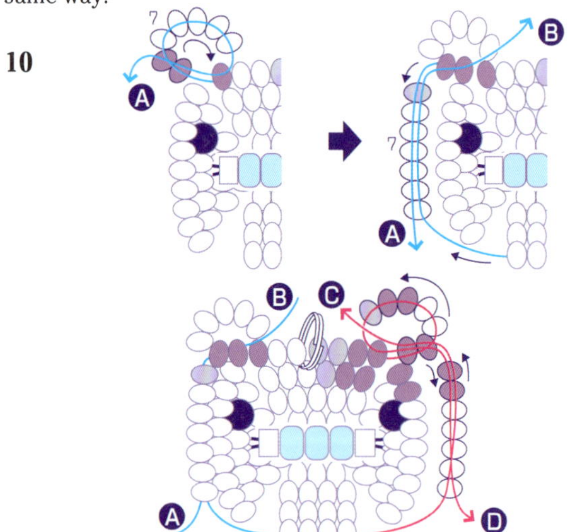

11. **Make back of head.** Twist A and B, and C and D wires together 3-4 times. Cut excess wire. After twisting the wire, fold ends under to prevent injury.

11
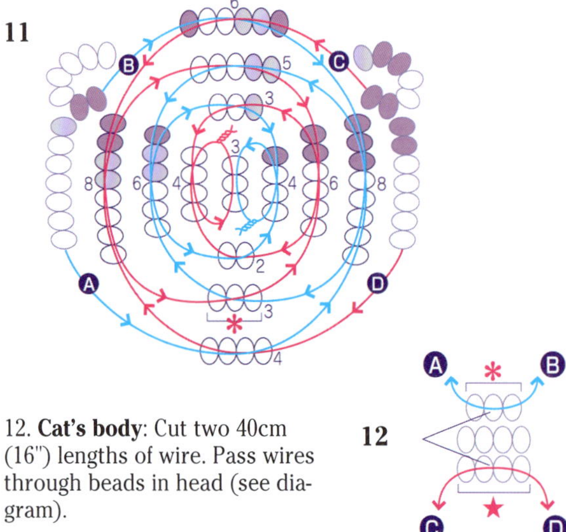

12. **Cat's body**: Cut two 40cm (16") lengths of wire. Pass wires through beads in head (see diagram).

12
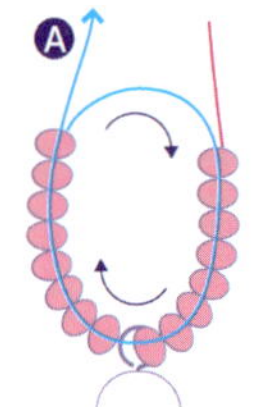

13

13. Continue making body. String bell on wire together with beads.

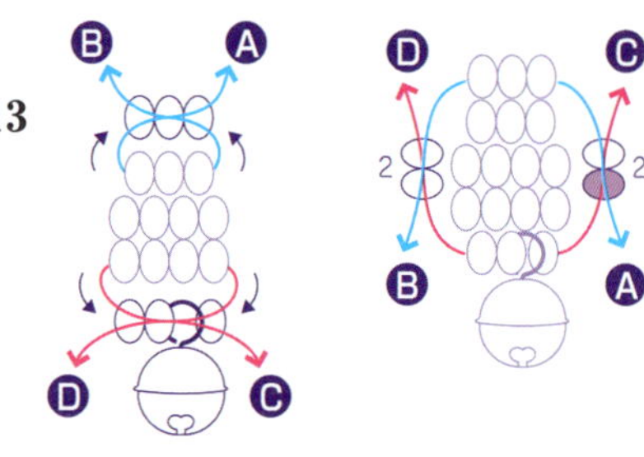

14. String beads for front legs and body, referring to diagrams.

14
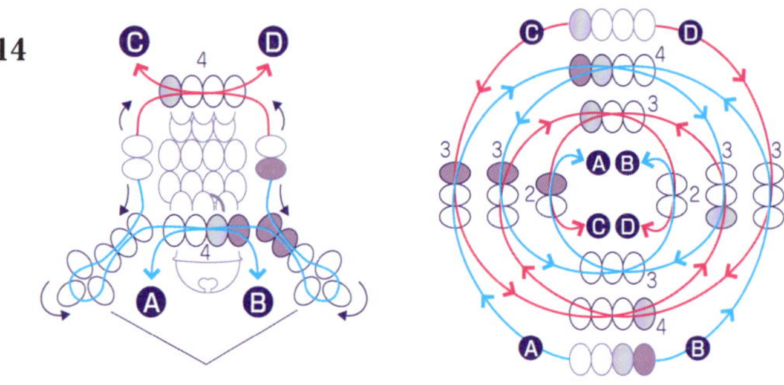

15. **Make hind legs and tail.** Twist A and C, and B and D wires together 3-4 times. Cut excess wire. After twisting the wire, fold ends under to prevent injury.

15
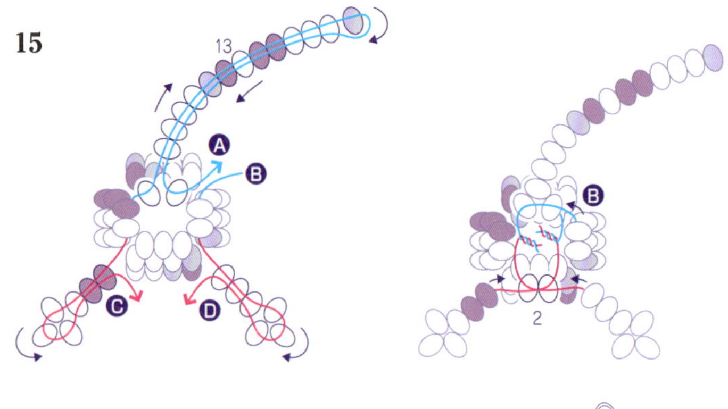

16. **Collar**: Pass 20cm (8") wire through bell. **16**
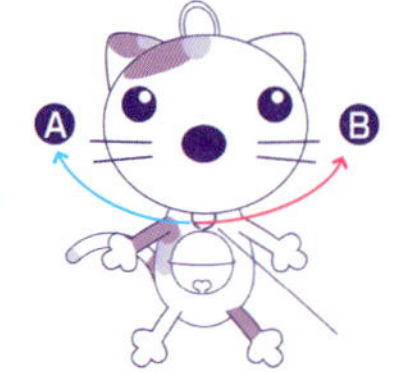

17. Add seed beads. Wrap collar around cat's neck. Pull wires and twist together 3-4 times. Cut excess wire. After twisting the wire, fold ends under to prevent injury.

17
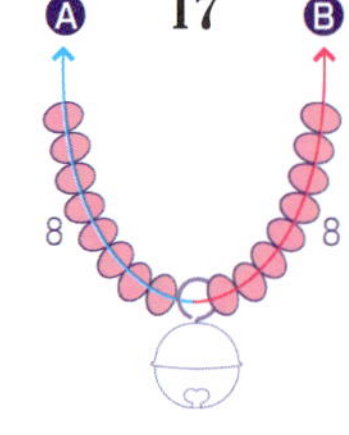

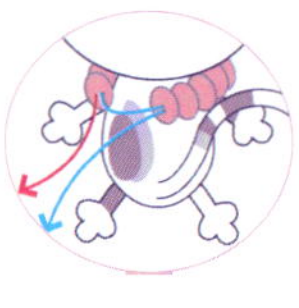

18. Adjust shape of cat. Insert key chain into split ring. See page 2 for adding the split ring.

Singing on a beautifully flowered branch, this bright bird is showing off his plumage for all to admire.

Materials:
Toho 11/0 seed beads (Yellow #42, Red #388, Pink #145F, Green #354, Brown #2152)
Toho 3mm Brown #222 bugle beads
7mm White acrylic bead with large hole
10mm White acrylic bead with large hole
Toho 3mm Black #PB-313 pop beads
Toho Pink #PB-784 flower pop bead
Toho Green #a-2384 leaf bead
32 Gauge gold wire • Split ring • Head pin
• Key chain • #2 nylon thread

1. **Bird's beak**: String beads on 20cm (8") nylon thread, referring to diagrams. Apply glue to knot. Hide thread ends in beads. Cut excess.

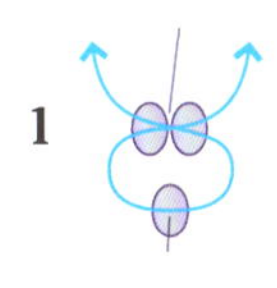

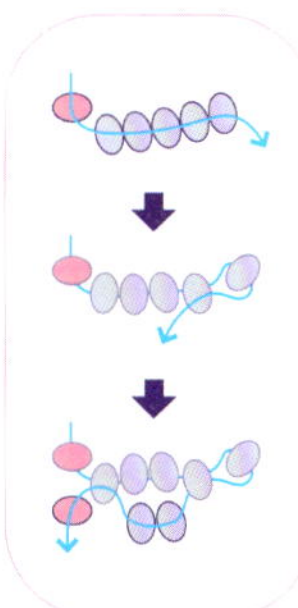

2. **Bird's head**: Tape 70cm (28") nylon thread down to work surface 8cm away from end. Pass thread through 10mm acrylic bead.

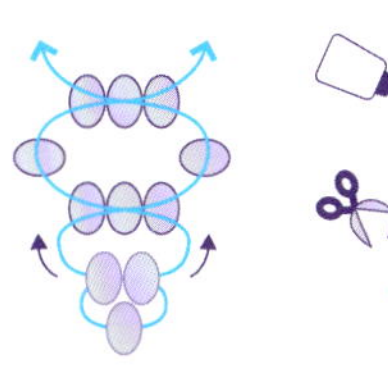

3. With taped end at the bottom, string beads on thread, wrapping it around 10mm bead.

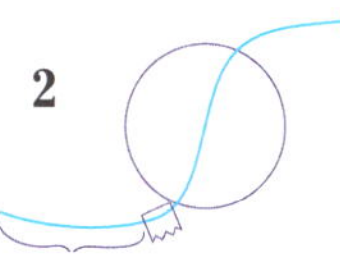

4. Continue stringing beads as in Step 2, paying careful attention to number and color. String beads in direction indicated by arrow in diagram. Attach beak made in Step 1 to Rows 4 and 6. Shape face as you work.

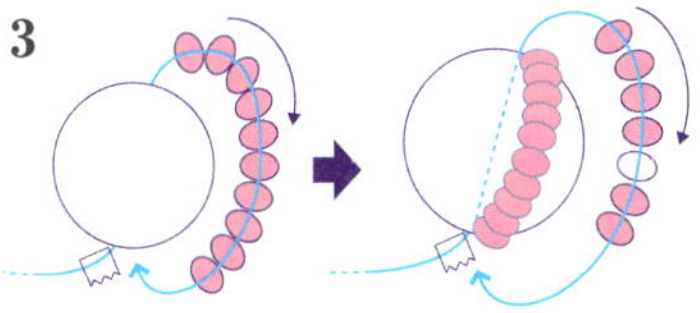

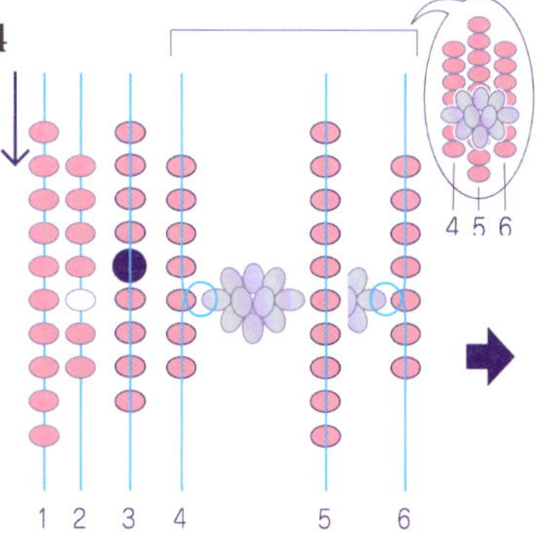

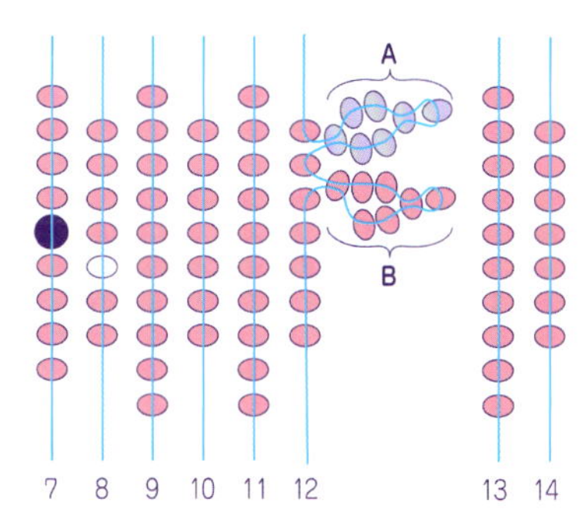

5. If a large area of the 10mm bead shows through after you've strung the beads for Row 14, add more rows until the bead is covered.

6. After you've strung the beads for the last row, pass thread through beads in Row 1. Tie thread to end left at starting point.

7. Remove tape at starting point. Tie threads together 2-3 times, and apply glue sparingly to knot.

8. Run thread ends through 2-3 beads. Cut excess.

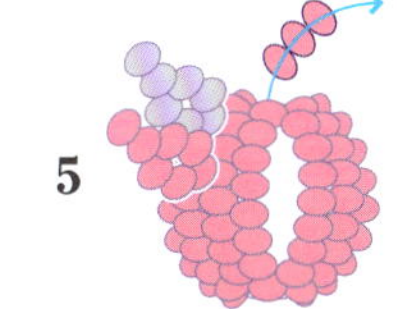

9. **Bird's body**: Use the 7mm acrylic bead and 50cm (20") nylon thread. The body is made in the same way as the head. After stringing beads for Row 11, finish in same way as Step 6.

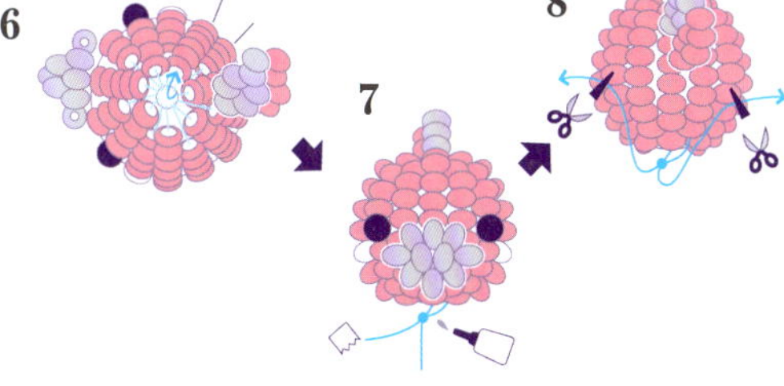

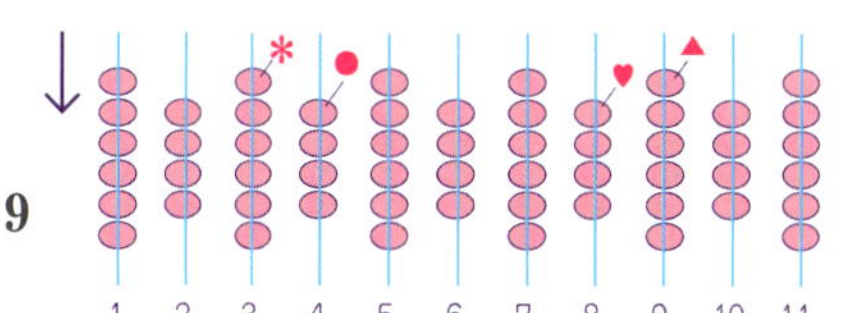

10. **Make tail** and attach to body.

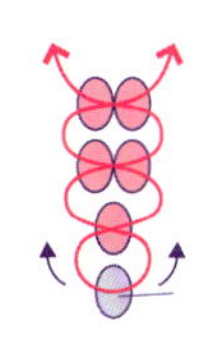

11. String beads on 15cm (6") wire.

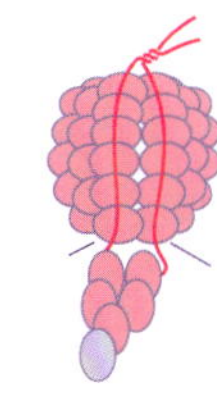

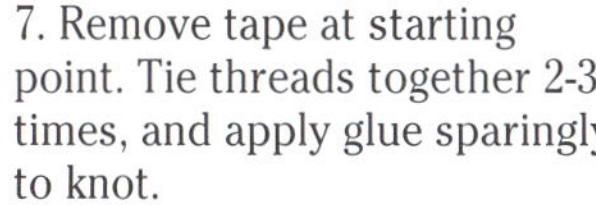

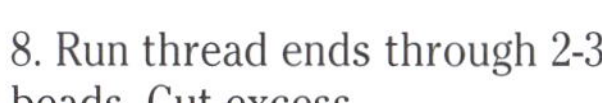

instructions continued on page 18

Bird instructions continued from page 17

12. Pass wire through beads in Rows 1 and 11 of body made in Step 9. Twist wire together 3-4 times. Cut excess.

12  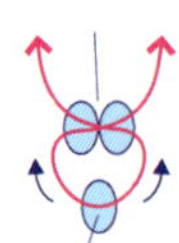 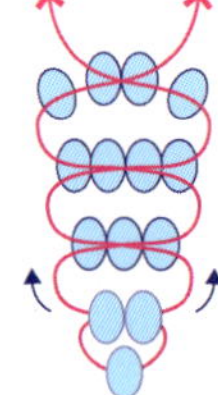

13. **Make wings and attach to body**: String beads on 15cm (6") wire to make wing.

13  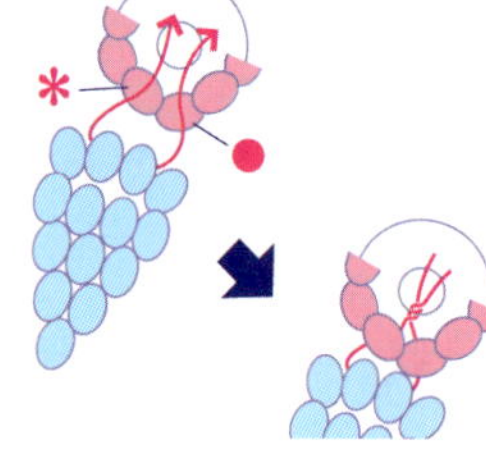

14 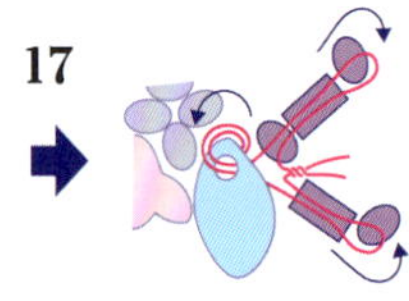

14. Pass wire through beads (see diagram) in Rows 3 and 4 of body made in Step 9. Twist wires together 3-4 times. Cut excess.

15. Make other wing in same way, this time passing wire through bead in Rows 8 and 9.

15

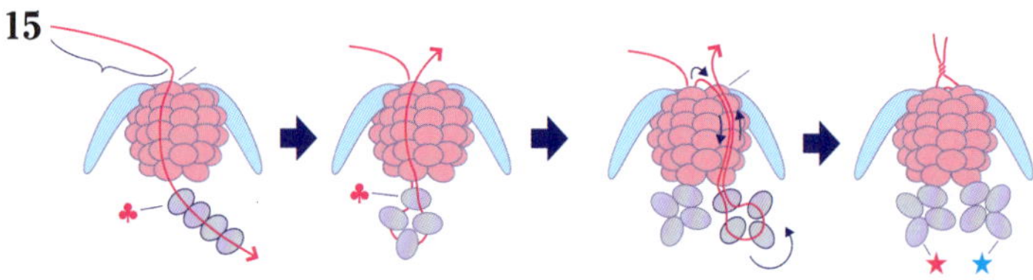

16. **Make feet and tree branch**: Leaving a 5cm (2") end, pass 15cm (6") wire through Rows 5 and 7 of body made in Step 9 to make feet. Twist ends of wire set aside earlier together 3-4 times. Cut excess.

16

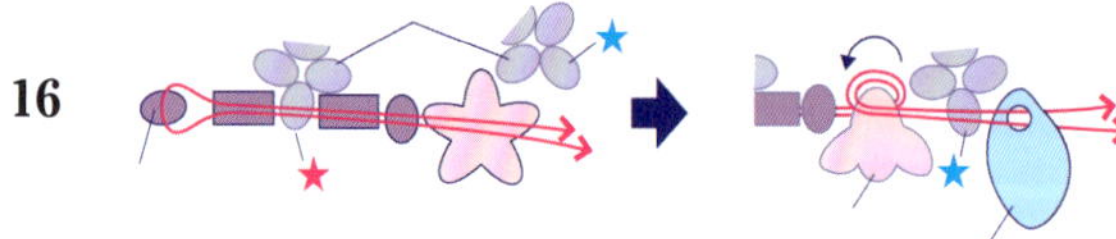

17

17. String beads on 30cm (12") wire, referring to drawings, to make tree branch. Twist wire together 3-4 times; cut excess.

18. Attach key chain. Cut shaft of head pin to 3cm. Insert head pin into body and head, in that order. Round end of head pin. See page 2 instructions Using Head Pins.

18

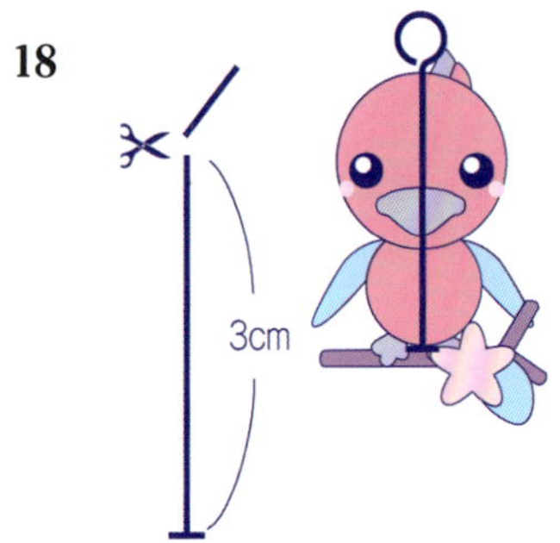

Beading fun is pure monkey business! This charming animal will have your friends making one too. After all, monkey see, monkey do.

Materials:
Toho 11/0 seed beads (Brown #34, Black #49, Beige #103, Red #5, Pink #908)
Toho 3mm Black #M49 magatama bead
7mm White acrylic bead with large hole
10mm White acrylic bead with large hole
Toho 3mm Black #PB-313 pop beads
Split ring • Head pin • Key chain • Nylon thread

1

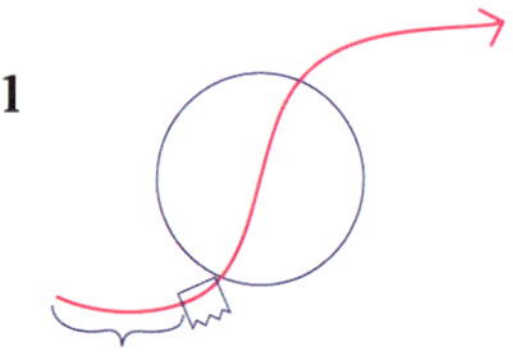

1. **Monkey's head**: Tape 70cm (28") nylon thread down to work surface 8cm (3") away from end. Pass other end of thread through 10mm acrylic bead.

2

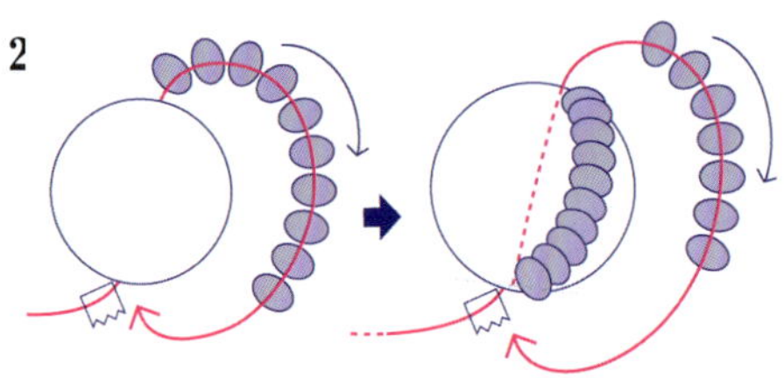

2. With taped end at the bottom, string beads on thread, wrapping them around 10mm bead.